COMMUNICATIVE GRAMMAR PRACTICE

Leo Jones

TEACHER'S MANUAL

CAMBRIDGE
UNIVERSITY PRESS

Published by the Press Syndicate of the University of Cambridge
The Pitt Building, Trumpington Street, Cambridge CB2 1RP
40 West 20th Street, New York, NY 10011-4211, USA
10 Stamford Road, Oakleigh, Victoria 3166, Australia

© Cambridge University Press 1992

First published 1992

Printed in the United States of America

ISBN 0 521 39890 8   (Teacher's Manual)
ISBN 0 521 39891 6   (Student's Book)

Book design: Peter Ducker

Contents

Contents

Introduction

Aims

Communicative Grammar Practice is a book of activities and exercises for intermediate students who:

- still make many grammatical errors
- lack confidence in using English in conversation and in writing
- feel safer using only the simplest grammatical structures
- find it difficult to use a variety of structures
- need to improve their spoken and written English for a forthcoming examination

By using the activities and exercises in this book, students will:

- improve their accuracy in speech and writing
- develop a feeling for accuracy
- learn to correct their own errors
- use English more creatively in communicative activities and tasks
- extend their range of expression

The book covers the main "problem areas" of English grammar and usage that students require at this level, including those tested in the Test of English as a Foreign Language (TOEFL), the Michigan Tests, and most standard examinations covering English grammar.

Activities and exercises

Each unit in *Communicative Grammar Practice* contains a variety of activities – some closely controlled, others more open-ended. Some of the activities may be done orally; others may be done in writing, sometimes after a brief discussion. Several different aspects of a grammatical area and different uses of the same forms are covered in each unit; therefore, the activities do not necessarily lead in to each other. The contrast between different kinds of activities within the same unit will help to maintain students' motivation throughout the lesson.

Communicative Grammar Practice is a grammar practice course that, by using English in different activities, allows students to discover in which areas of English they are strong and weak – and then sets out to improve their weaknesses. Most of the grammar involved will already have come up in previous, more elementary classes and will have been experienced in reading or listening material. There is, therefore, no explicit presentation of new structures in each unit.

The first activity in the unit usually sets the scene for the activities that follow, by means of a short dialogue, some illustrated examples, or an introductory practice exercise. Any explanation of grammatical points should arise naturally from the questions students ask – and from the errors they make. Students must be encouraged to participate in this process, to ask questions if they are puzzled, and not to sit back and expect to be "taught" to use English accurately.

Using this book

Communicative Grammar Practice is designed to be used as the grammar practice component of a balanced course for intermediate students. Any students who need to improve their grammatical accuracy will find the material in this book both useful and enjoyable. For example, it is suitable:

- for students who need to learn and practice English grammar at an intermediate level
- for students who need to review English grammar

1

– as a preliminary course in grammatical accuracy for students who will later be using more advanced material that presupposes a good knowledge of English grammar
– for students who need to improve their spoken and written accuracy and who are taking the TOEFL or a similar exam
– for students who are also using other material that emphasizes oral fluency and listening skills, such as *Great Ideas* by Leo Jones and Victoria Kimbrough (Cambridge University Press)

It is not necessary to work through *Communicative Grammar Practice* systematically unit by unit from beginning to end, even though the earlier units are less advanced than the later ones. You will need to decide what your particular class's weaknesses are and concentrate on the units covering these areas. Although a more advanced class may benefit from "dipping into" the material here and there, the average intermediate student will find that most of the material is relevant and useful, though every activity will probably not need to be studied for an equal length of time. The order of the units in the book can be changed according to the needs of a particular class, but it is recommended that two-part units be done in sequence (e.g., Unit 8 should be done only after Unit 7).

As a teacher, you have an essential role to play in correcting errors and encouraging self-correction. Everyone learning a language makes mistakes, and it takes time for these to be eliminated. Many difficulties are unforeseeable: They may be personal to an individual student, or they may be particular to the student's language background. *Communicative Grammar Practice* attempts to identify problem areas and to provide plenty of practice material for you to use in your class. But it cannot anticipate all the errors everyone is going to make. This Teacher's Manual will help you make the most of the material in the Student's Book, but you will also need the active participation of your students to succeed fully.

Each unit requires approximately 45 to 90 minutes to cover in class. The exact time you need will depend on how many exercises you assign as homework, whether you use any supplementary activities, and, above all, on the level of your class. You may need to spend more or less time on particular units according to your class's particular "problem areas" in English grammar – and some units may be skipped altogether if they deal with areas that are no problem for your students.

The teacher and the class

Most of the activities in *Communicative Grammar Practice* are designed to be done by students working together in small groups or in pairs. In some cases, particularly in small classes and in situations where you want to closely monitor accuracy, activities can be done as a whole class. Either way, students should be urged to explore and experiment with their English, and not just work through the exercises mechanically as if they were drills. If students can only fill in blanks in exercises, or only write sentences, they aren't going to be successful in using English as a means of communication. Only by using English creatively can students develop their ability to actually use English to express their own ideas.

If students are corrected all the time, they will feel vulnerable when they speak. The atmosphere in class should be relaxed and cooperative, not tense and competitive. In this way, students are more likely to enjoy their lessons, acquire more English, and make progress.

Some of these ideas may help to develop a relaxed and cooperative atmosphere in the classroom:

– Try to make students feel that you value their ideas and contributions – and encourage them to value each other's contributions too.
– Encourage each individual to contribute to the class – treat everyone as a responsible adult (especially if your students are teenagers), not as a "kid."
– Try not to talk too much – the more you speak the less time your students have to speak themselves.
– Address the class as you would address a

group of colleagues, rather than an "audience."

- Don't stand up all the time, otherwise you'll always seem to be the center of attention.
- Encourage students to regard you as a guide, adviser, and facilitator whose role is to organize the class so that they can practice and use the language points they are studying, and to help them to learn.

Before starting an activity, it is always helpful to put yourself in your students' shoes and ask yourself these questions:

- What would it be like to be doing this activity or exercise? What would I enjoy about it? What would I find difficult?
- What's the purpose of the activity? If it's not obvious, you may need to explain it to your students, rather than expect them to do it just because you want them to.
- Do your students know how long they have to complete the activity?

After each activity make sure you allow time for feedback. Tell the class about any errors you noted. Encourage them to ask questions on grammar points and vocabulary.

Working in pairs or groups

Many of the activities and exercises in *Communicative Grammar Practice* are designated as Pair Work or Group Work. It may be necessary to rearrange the seats in your classroom to provide a convenient atmosphere for this. Try to make sure the class isn't always arranged in rows with the teacher standing at the front, or always as a horseshoe with the teacher as the focus of everyone's attention. It's better if the students' chairs can be arranged in a circle – they'll be able to see each other better, and you'll be able to circulate easily around the class while they're working in pairs or groups.

There are many advantages to having students work together in pairs or small groups:

- Every student gets an opportunity to communicate with another – in a whole-class situation, it tends to be the quickest or loudest students whose ideas dominate.

- Students feel less inhibited, and they are more willing to experiment with their English – they don't "play it safe" by using the simplest vocabulary and structures as they might do when "performing" in front of the whole class. Shy, quiet students often become quite talkative when they're in small groups.
- Students are more likely to remember answers they've discovered or worked out by themselves than other students' answers – or answers the teacher announces to the class.
- Students working in groups are more active than when they are working as a class: They talk and think more. If a class of, say, twenty were doing a ten-question exercise "around the class," half of them wouldn't even have the opportunity to answer a question.
- Even if students are simply doing a fill-in-the-blanks exercise together, this task provides them with opportunities to communicate naturally together in English while they're doing it – just as if they were doing a problem-solving task or a discussion activity together.

The teacher's role during such activities is to move around the class from pair to pair or group to group:

- eavesdropping on each pair or group (and, while doing so, discouraging students from using their native language – reminding them that they can make progress only by speaking English together in class)
- showing an interest
- offering suggestions and advice
- making notes of "relevant errors" you overhear to be discussed afterwards (see Correction and "Relevant Errors" on page 5)
- keeping track of the progress of the activity and deciding when to call a halt

To discourage students from talking in their native language during these activities, make sure they know and use simple interactional phrases like these when working together:

OK, let's start.
How do you say "..." in English?
Whose turn is it?
You should have said "..."
Can you move your chair?

Let's look it up in the dictionary.
I think we're finished.
What do we have to do?
I don't understand this word.
It's your turn.
What did you say?
What do you think the answer is?
I'll ask the teacher about that.
What should we do now?

It's a good idea to go over these phrases with the class at the beginning of the course – and maybe review them during the course too! If possible, post them prominently in the classroom for easy reference anytime and ongoing review.

Doing activities in pairs or groups usually takes more time than doing them as a whole class. However, some of the exercises can be done as homework, which saves time. Homework can be checked in class with students comparing their answers in pairs or groups, and discussing as a class any problems they encountered.

Even the activities where students are expected to write their answers (see Writing on this page) can be done by students working together. The collaboration involved in producing a set of answers, or a solution to a problem, is both enjoyable and beneficial. Sometimes, however, to provide variety or a change of pace, you may prefer to ask students to do such exercises alone – or to do them for homework.

There are advantages and disadvantages of students' having a "regular partner" in class. On the one hand, a regular pair can become an efficient working team who enjoy each other's company, enjoy speaking English together, and stimulate each other; on the other hand, regular partners may run out of ideas and grow tired of each other and, if they aren't well matched, may slow each other down. It makes sense, therefore, to have students change partners regularly, giving everyone a chance to be everyone else's partner at some point during the course. This can be done easily by saying to the class: "I think it'd be a good idea for all of you to have a new partner. So will everyone stand up and go find a person you haven't spoken to for a while and then sit together?"

Writing

Communicative Grammar Practice includes many exercises to be done in writing. In some units there are several of these, which may involve writing sentences, filling in blanks, making notes, or writing short paragraphs.

Writing is an extremely valuable way of developing accuracy, and, as previously suggested, it needn't be a solitary activity. Most students find that writing helps them focus their attention and remember better, and if your students find writing helpful in this way you may want to introduce writing tasks into some of the oral activities.

At least one writing exercise in each unit (usually the last exercise) can be assigned for homework. This will help consolidate what students have practiced in class. Students who are unwilling to do homework may need to be persuaded that it will help them to remember what they've done in class. Besides, none of the writing exercises in *Communicative Grammar Practice* are very long! However, if preferred, the exercises can be done in class in writing – by students working alone or cooperating in pairs.

Accuracy and fluency

It seems clear that a *balanced* approach, where both fluency and accuracy are developed, is essential if students are to do more than simply "survive" in English-speaking situations. For example, a student who is only going to use English in informal conversations with good friends (who may be willing to ignore grammatical errors) may not need to improve her or his accuracy. But students who need to participate in conversations with English-speaking strangers or with English-speaking colleagues can't "get by" all the time by speaking fluent, inaccurate English (though most people are happy to tolerate a foreign accent and occasional errors). Very inaccurate speakers may even find that people are listening to their mistakes, not to what they're trying to say!

In writing, inaccuracy is a greater handicap, because errors are far more noticeable to a reader than they are to a listener. And, of course, students whose writing contains many errors are likely to do poorly on most English examinations.

Communicative Grammar Practice not only provides practice material for students who need to improve their accuracy in speech and in writing, but it also contains activities that will help students develop both accuracy *and* fluency by giving them opportunities to communicate in English.

Students need to learn to monitor their own accuracy. Writing, unlike speech, can be performed at an individual's own speed and, thus, affords students the opportunity to notice more errors. Care must be taken, however, that students don't become *preoccupied* with accuracy, as this would hinder fluent communication. A student who is preoccupied with accuracy is unlikely to be able to use English very well in conversation if we define accuracy as "not making mistakes" and fluency as "communicating in spite of one's limited knowledge of English and the errors one may be making."

Correction and "relevant errors"

Students can't suddenly and miraculously achieve accuracy in spoken English. The best that can be hoped for is a progressive improvement in accuracy. Correction is an essential tool to guide students toward improvement, but there is no point in correcting every single error made. Instead, you should concentrate on correcting "relevant errors" – those connected with the theme of the unit: for example, verb forms in Unit 3 and prepositions in Unit 15, but not vice versa.

Some examples of "typical" relevant errors are listed at the beginning of each unit in this Teacher's Manual. The examples are given for guidance only so that teachers may be aware of the *kinds* of error that should be corrected. The *actual* errors students make can vary widely, depending on their language background. There is no need for students to be made aware of the typical errors listed in the Teacher's Manual.

Correcting errors calls for gentleness and tact. Sensitive or diffident students often feel they are being reprimanded or even mocked if told they are "wrong." Even well-adjusted, confident students can be upset by aggressive correction. Thus, correction should be regarded as a *positive* act designed to help students improve their accuracy – never as an implied criticism. In fact, rather than announcing a correction to a student, or even saying "No that's not quite right," encourage self-correction. This can be done good-naturedly as the following examples show.

Student: *What you did yesterday?*
Teacher: *Pardon?*
Student: *I mean: What did you do yesterday?*

Student: *I enjoy to watch TV.*
Teacher: [raises eyebrows or lifts forefinger slightly to indicate error]
Student: *Er . . . I enjoy watching TV.*

Student: *I'm interested for baseball.*
Teacher: *Interested for?*
Student: *No, I mean, interested in baseball.*

If such techniques fail, the conversation can continue and other members of the group or class can be asked to suggest a correction, like this:

Student: *I've seen her yesterday.*
Teacher: *Excuse me?*
Student: *I said: I've seen her yesterday.*
Teacher: *Well, that's not quite right. Can anyone help?*

Provided that this kind of peer correction is offered in a friendly and helpful way, it can be a very effective correction technique.

Sometimes, however, you can save time by offering a correction after the student has had a chance at self-correction. Again, this should be done kindly and tactfully by saying, for example, "I think you mean you *saw* her yesterday" or "It's probably better to say: 'If I *were* you.'" The important thing to get across is that it's not the *person* who's wrong, but his or her *English* that's wrong.

During pair work and group work you should be moving constantly from pair to pair or group to group. Sometimes it may be necessary to interrupt to encourage self-correction (saying

"Pardon" or "Excuse me" as suggested in the preceding dialogues). Often, however, such interruptions may be unwelcome or intrusive, and correction should not occur while students are still concentrating on the activity. You should *make notes* of the "relevant errors" you overhear as you move around the class. After the activity has finished, write those errors on the board and ask students to suggest corrections. The students who made the errors needn't be identified if you begin: "I heard someone say . . ." or "One of you said . . ." or "What's wrong with this sentence: . . .?"

This kind of *feedback* session is essential after each activity, but you should remember to encourage and praise the class as well as criticize them. It's so much more motivating to hear "That was really good! Good job!" than "Now, here are the mistakes you made . . ." This feedback session also gives students a chance to ask any questions about the language (especially vocabulary) they need in order to perform the activity better, and, as already emphasized, such questions should be encouraged.

You should treat written work in a similar way: underline, rather than correct, relevant errors so that students have to make their own corrections. If students can't improve some parts of their work, they should ask a partner for help before consulting you. As with spoken English, you should concentrate on relevant errors, encouraging self-correction of these. Other errors can simply be noted by writing the correct form above the incorrect word or phrase. The following example is part of a paragraph written in Unit 3, so the relevant errors are those connected with verb forms. (Written work of this type should be done on alternate lines to allow plenty of space for self-correction later.)

Mary <u>were</u> walking down the street
one
~~on~~ day when she <u>see</u> some money
lying on
~~lieing in~~ the sidewalk. She <u>look</u>
around to see if anyone <u>is</u> watching
her but they <u>didn't</u>.

Communication activities

Some of the activities in *Communicative Grammar Practice* are called Communication Activities. Their purpose is to stimulate real conversation as much as possible. When we are talking to another person, we don't always know what information the other person has or what the other person is going to say. In other words, there is an "information gap." In the communication activities, students are directed to separate sections at the back of the book, where each person is given different information and can't see the other's information. The object is for students to find out what their partners know and to tell their partners what they know. In this way an "information gap" is created and bridged – and communication takes place.

In these activities each student has a "task" to perform and has to *use* the information she or he receives. Students will find that they are strongly motivated by their desire to receive, offer, and exchange information and by the realism and value of the tasks themselves.

As students do the communication activities, you can go around the room and make yourself available for help with vocabulary, instructions, and corrections, as needed. Remind students not to look at each other's information – if they need to find out what their partners are looking at, they should ask them questions.

Most of the communication activities call for pair work. If there's an odd number of students in your class, you should form one group of three, with two of the students sharing one set of information and working as a team. You should not participate to make an even pair, because you need to monitor the activity.

There is a description of each Communication Activity in this Teacher's Manual and a complete index on page 8.

Using the Teacher's Manual

At the beginning of each unit in this Teacher's Manual is a Grammar Summary with examples of the points covered in the unit – there is a slightly simplified version of these Grammar Summaries on pages 66–80 in the Student's Book. The summaries give an overview of the grammar involved, but they are not intended as a substitute for the complete explanations that a grammar reference book might give. Teachers who need the reassurance of a more complete description of grammar and usage should refer to Raymond Murphy's *Grammar in Use* (Cambridge University Press).

After the Grammar Summary in each unit is a list of Relevant Errors. These are examples of the kind of errors students might make while doing the activities and exercises in the unit – see Correction and "Relevant Errors" on page 5. These are not necessarily the actual errors your students will make.

Most sections within a unit begin with "Warm-up": These are ideas for introducing the activity or exercise to the class.

A suggested Procedure follows, describing how to handle the activity or exercise in class. There are also Answers or Sample/Suggested Answers, if appropriate. In cases where more than one correct answer is possible, students should be encouraged to have a tolerance for several options. There are often many different ways of saying the same thing in English, and none of them is necessarily "the best one."

Finally there are Follow-up ideas – these range from straightforward discussion questions to longer supplementary activities that you can introduce to add variety or a change of pace to the lesson.

The notes for Unit 1 are more detailed than those for subsequent units and contain an explanation of some of the principles underlying the activities in this book. After you've done the first unit with your class, a quick re-read of this introduction is recommended, so that you feel at home with the techniques you'll be using in later units.

I hope you like using *Communicative Grammar Practice* with your class!

Index of the Communication Activities in the Student's Book

1 | Yes/No questions

Grammar summary

The various activities in this unit cover the following grammar points. For a detailed explanation of the rules involved and more examples, consult *Grammar in Use* by Raymond Murphy (Cambridge University Press) or a similar reference book.

There is a slightly simplified version of this summary on page 66 of the Student's Book.

Practice in forming and using *Yes/No* questions, which usually end with a rising intonation:

Are *you* **feeling** *all right?*
Is *this correct?*
Did *you* **go** *to the park in the afternoon?*
Can *I* **help** *you?*
Have *you ever* **eaten** *lobster?*
Were *you in class yesterday?*
Do *you* **play** *tennis?*

Using negative questions with rising intonation (showing that the speaker is fairly certain but is making sure that she or he is right):

Isn't *that your brother?*
Isn't *this correct?*
Can't *you* **swim?**
Didn't *she once* **live** *in Tokyo?*
Aren't *you* **feeling** *well?*
Haven't *you* **finished** *yet?*

Relevant errors

"Relevant errors" are errors directly connected with the theme of the unit (see page 5). Whenever possible, encourage students to correct themselves, if they can, before you offer your own corrections. It's unlikely that any class will make all the errors listed here. Rather, the following list shows the *kind* of errors that should be corrected if they are made during the activities in this unit.

✗ Play you tennis?
✗ Was you in class yesterday?
✗ You have ever eaten lobster?
✗ Don't you can swim?
✗ Went you to the park in the afternoon?

Students should also be corrected if they don't use appropriate intonation in their questions.

1.1 Do you like . . . ?

Warm-up (*3–5 minutes*)

Books are closed. Tell the class about a few of the foods you like and don't like. For example:

Olives are one of my favorite foods. I really like them. But I don't like raisins. I never eat them.

Then call on various students to see if they share your likes and dislikes:

Carlos, do you like raisins?

Encourage students to answer "Yes, I do" or "No, I don't." If they are comfortable with this structure, encourage them to elaborate on their answers:

No, I don't like raisins, but I like grapes.
No, I don't like raisins at all. They're awful!

When students understand the structures involved in this activity, move on to the procedure.

Procedure

A   Books are open. Look at the list as a class. Make sure everyone understands all the categories. Then have students fill in the list, while you go around the class giving help with vocabulary as needed.

Make sure everyone has completed most of the list before starting part B. This shouldn't take too long. If students can't think of *three* movie titles, for example, one is enough for this activity.

B *Group work* Arrange the class into groups of 3 or 4. The members of each group ask each other questions to find out about the others' likes and dislikes. Circulate around the class, showing an interest and taking notes of relevant errors, but interrupting only if absolutely necessary. This is a very straightforward activity, and there should be few mistakes in grammar (although there may be some questions about vocabulary).

Encourage everyone to speak in English *all* the time during the group work. Write the useful expressions that are listed on pages 3 and 4 of this Teacher's Manual on the board (*OK, let's start, What do we have to do?*, etc.). This will help students use English even when they're deciding what to do. You could also write the expressions on large sheets of paper and hang these around the classroom for use in future class sessions.

Follow-up

If your class found the activity in part B fairly easy, write these phrases on the board:

I'd like to know if . . .
Could you tell me if . . .

Students then redo the conversation in part B (maybe with rearranged groups) using these more polite forms. Students should imagine they are talking to people they don't know well:

I'd like to know if pizza is one of your favorite foods.
Could you tell me if you have toast for breakfast?

If there's time, have students ask each other *why* they like or dislike the things they mention. For example:

Student A: *Why don't you like lemonade?*

Student B: *It's too sour.* OR *I don't care for the taste.*

1.2 In the news

Warm-up (*2–3 minutes*)

Books are closed. Begin by getting the class to ask you some questions about yourself. Encourage them to ask *Yes/No* questions. For example:

Student 1: *Are you Canadian?*
Teacher: *Yes, I am. Are you Canadian?*
Student 1: *No, I'm not. I'm Japanese.*
Student 2: *Do you like rock music?*
Teacher: *Yes, I do. Do you?*
Student 2: (etc.)

Other possible questions are:

Can you speak Spanish?
Have you ever been abroad?
Do you like to travel?
Is Portuguese your native language?
Can you swim?
Do you play golf?

Procedure

A Books are open. Ask the class to suggest some questions that the reporters might be asking, using the words in parts B and C. For example, here are some questions the reporter in the first picture might be asking:

Do you feel proud?
Have you done this before?
Has this been a valuable experience?
Are you tired?
Will you climb any other mountains?
Was the mountain hard to climb?
Did the climb take very long?
Did you leave early in the morning?

B *Pair work* While students are writing their questions together, circulate around the class looking at their work and offering advice and corrections where necessary. The purpose of this exercise is to use the correct structures and word order.

C Having written their ten questions for part B, students now add five more questions, beginning with *Did . . . ?* Then have everyone trade lists with another pair to compare ideas and perhaps suggest improvements. Allow time for pairs to give each other feedback.

D Rearrange the class so that everyone has a new partner. Now ask pairs to role-play two or three of the interviews, taking turns as the reporter. Circulate around the class, showing an interest and taking note of relevant errors, but interrupting only if absolutely necessary.

Finally, spend a few minutes giving the class feedback. Point out any relevant errors you noted and ask the class to suggest corrections.

Follow-up

Using "short answers" quickly and accurately is a challenge for students. It isn't easy for them to catch, retain, and respond with the correct forms while processing the meaning. Spend some time in rapid, gamelike practice:

Do you feel proud?
– Yes, I do.
Have you achieved what you wanted to do?
– No, I haven't.
Has this been a valuable experience?
– Yes, it has.
Are you feeling tired now?
– No, I'm not.   (etc.)

To keep the practice moving at a good pace, jot down a fairly extensive list of questions beforehand to serve as a cue card. Repeat the practice, or parts of it, two or three times if needed for students to perform confidently and well.

1.3   Yes or No?

Warm-up (*3–5 minutes*)

Books are closed. Tell the class that you are a famous person (e.g., Christopher Columbus, Abraham Lincoln, Marie Curie), but don't tell them who you are. If you are teaching in your students' own country, try to use a famous

historical figure from their own culture. Get them to ask you *Yes/No* questions in order to guess who you are. Questions they might ask include:

Were you very famous?
Did you live a long time ago?
Are you still alive?
Did you discover something?

Once students seem comfortable asking these kinds of questions, move on to the procedure.

Procedure

Pair work   Make sure students know what they have to do. Allow a little time for them to think of some people, and help those who lack inspiration by whispering ideas to them. Students should secretly write down the names of their famous people. (If your students are likely to have trouble thinking of people, this step could be done as homework to save time in class.)

While the class is doing this activity, go around listening to as many pairs as possible. When they have finished, or have had enough, ask some students to challenge the rest of the class to guess the name of their famous people.

Follow-up

Give the class further practice in asking *Yes/No* questions by playing this well-known game: One student volunteers to be the "contestant." The class then asks the contestant *Yes/No* questions. The contestant, however, must avoid saying "yes" or "no." This can be done by saying things like "That's true," "Absolutely," or "I don't think so" for as long as possible. If the contestant accidentally says "yes" or "no," he or she is out of the game, and the person who asked the last question becomes the contestant.

Here are some *Yes/No* questions that might be asked:

Are you feeling OK?
Are you wearing a red sweater?
Do you have brown hair?
Did you stay up late last night?
Is it Tuesday today?

A whistle, bell, or buzzer can be used to give the right kind of "game show" atmosphere. Blow the whistle, ring the bell, or sound the buzzer to start each round and again when a contestant says "yes" or "no."

1.4 Communication activity: Photographs

Warm-up

As this is the first Communication Activity, explain the purpose and the procedure students should follow (see Communication Activities on page 6).

Tell the students: "In this activity you will work in groups of three. Each of you will have different information – in this case different photographs. The idea is to find out about the other photos by asking each other questions. But you can only find out by asking questions: You shouldn't look at your partners' photos."

Procedure

Group work   Arrange the class into groups of three. Student A should look at Activity 1 on page 81 in the Student's Book. Student B should look at Activity 5 on page 82. Student C should look at Activity 12 on page 85.

Each student has a different photograph. Remind them not to look at each other's pictures. The idea is for students to find out what is happening in each other's pictures by asking *Yes/No* questions. For example:

Are there any people in the picture?
Are they wearing dressy clothes?
Are they indoors?
Are the people talking to each other?

While groups are doing the activity, go around the class eavesdropping. Make sure students are doing what they are supposed to do and are not looking at each other's pictures. After the activity is over, students can look at each other's pictures.

Finally, describe as a class what's going on in each of the pictures, asking various class members to contribute sentences.

Follow-up

Choose whichever of these follow-up activities seems more suitable for your class. Activity B involves more writing.

A

1. Prepare a set of picture cards made from photos cut out of magazines and mounted on cardboard. Find photos that are interesting (e.g., that show several different actions) and easy to describe.
2. Then, with the class divided into pairs, hand each student a picture.
3. Each student asks his or her partner questions to find out as much as possible about the other's picture. The photos should not be shown until the questioner has built up a fairly full image of what is in the picture.
4. When a pair has finished, give them two more picture cards or get them to trade with another pair.

B
Variation of activity A: When a questioner has built up a fairly full image of what is in the unseen picture (after step 3), his or her partner shows the photo. Then each writes a description of the photo. When the pair are done, they can show each other and compare their written descriptions.

1.5 Making sure

Procedure

This exercise is a warm-up for Exercise 1.6 and provides practice forming negative questions. It can be done by students working alone or collaborating in pairs.

ANSWERS
4. **Haven't** you changed your hairstyle?
5. **Didn't** you use to have long hair?

6. **Weren't** you wearing a blue sweater that night?
7. **Wasn't** your car damaged or something?
8. **Didn't** you have to leave suddenly?

Follow-up

Look at the illustration and questions on page 3 in the Student's Book. Ask the class these questions:

How well do the speakers know each other?
What may have happened after the conversation took place?

1.6   Didn't you go to the movies?

Warm-up *(2 minutes)*

Books are closed. Talk to the class, pretending that you are trying to remember some information about each of them.

Ana, don't you come from the south of the country?
Yoshio, didn't you arrive here in January?
Kim, weren't you late for class last Friday?
(etc.)

Ana, Yoshio, and Kim should answer the questions – or the whole class can join the discussion.

Procedure

A   *Pair work*   Books are open. It's important that students rely on their memories in this activity, in order to simulate an authentic "making sure" situation (the point of the exercise is not for students to accurately remember every piece of information, but to use language in trying to remember). Remind them that they should only *talk* in part A – they *write* later on in part B.

You can control the questioning by writing this table on the board.

Last week	*Morning*	*Afternoon*	*Evening*
Mon.			
Tues.			
Wed.			
Thurs.			
Fri.			
Sat.			
Sun.			

B   Separate the pairs. Ask students to make very brief, rough notes of what they found out from their partner.

C   *Pair work*   Reassemble the pairs so that they can make sure their notes are correct, following the pattern conversation in the Student's Book. If there are some activities they can't remember, they should "make up" some things to ask about, rather than say nothing.

Go around the class, making notes of relevant errors you overhear. Give the class feedback on their "performance" and ask them to correct the errors you point out.

Follow-up

1. Have students, working alone or in pairs, write a list of questions like these:

Didn't Tolstoy write Romeo and Juliet?
Didn't Madonna sing "I want to hold your hand"?
Didn't Nobel invent dynamite?

The questions can be about entertainment, sports, or whatever interests your students.
2. Then students ask a partner (or another pair) to answer the questions:

Didn't Tolstoy write Romeo and Juliet?
– *No, Shakespeare wrote it.*
Didn't Madonna sing "I want to hold your hand"?
– *No, that was the Beatles.*
Didn't Nobel invent dynamite?
– *Well, yes, I think he did.*

2 | *Wh- questions*

Grammar summary

Using a full range of *Wh-* question words:

What . . . ?	*Who . . . ?*	*Where . . . ?*
When . . . ?	*Which . . . ?*	*Why . . . ?*
How . . . ?	*How many . . . ?*	*How*
much . . . ?	*What . . . for?*	*What else . . . ?*

Practice in forming and using *Wh-* questions, which usually end with a falling intonation:

How many cookies **have** *you* **eaten***?*
Who **gave** *you the book?*
When **will** *you* **know***?*
What **did** *you* **do** *yesterday?*
Who **did** *you* **give** *the book* **to***?**
What time **does** *the flight* **leave***?*

*Some people prefer to use *whom* in these forms:
To whom *did you give the book?* OR **Whom** *did you give the book* **to?**
but they are more common in writing and not often used in conversation.

Using indirect question forms in polite questions:

Could you tell me **where** *the museum* **is***?*
I'd like to know **if** *you***'ve** *ever* **been** *to Korea.*
Would you mind telling me **what** *you* **did** *there?*

Relevant errors

Students should be corrected if they make errors like these during this unit:

✗ What you did yesterday?
✗ What means "outer space"?
✗ What does mean "planet"?
✗ What drank she?
✗ Who to did you give the book?
✗ Who you gave the book?

✗ What for you did that?
✗ What you are doing here?
✗ I'd like to know when are you leaving?
✗ Could you tell me do you understand?

They should also be corrected if they ask questions with inappropriate intonation.

2.1 Welcome to Earth!

Warm-up (*2 minutes*)

Look at the illustration on page 4 in the Student's Book as a class. Ask students to describe what is happening: An alien, or extraterrestrial, has landed on Earth from outer space. TV and newspaper reporters are asking "it" questions. Get students to say the *Wh-* words in the reporters' speech bubbles: *who, what, when, why, where, how*. These *Wh-* words usually start questions.

Procedure

A *Pair work* In pairs, students write down the questions that they think the reporters are asking. Here are just a few possible questions:

Who have you come to see?
Where have you come from?
What are your first impressions of our planet?
When are you planning to leave?
Why did you come?
How did you get here?
What are you going to do while you're here?
What else are you going to do here?

Alternatively, this can be done as a class activity, with everyone contributing questions.

(a)   (b)

Figure 2.1

B   If the class needs inspiration or challenge, put the whole list of *Wh-* question words on the board. Ask students to write at least one or, in some cases, two questions with each question word. Include *how far* and *how long* to make sure students aren't confusing these two expressions.

Then ask everyone to discuss in pairs what answers the visitor from outer space might give. Encourage students to use the following phrases, which are useful when we want to delay answering a question – to give us a little "thinking time":

Well, . . .
Let me see, . . .
Hmm . . . That's a very interesting question . . .

And these phrases, which are used when we can't answer the question at all:

I'm not really sure.
I don't really know.
I'm afraid I have no idea.
I can't answer that one – sorry.

When they are done, have students report back to the whole class.

Finally, divide the class into different pairs or groups of 3 and have them role-play an interview between the visitor from outer space and one or two reporters.

Follow-up

In this whole-class activity, students ask you questions and make a sketch according to your answers. The complete drawing is shown in Figure 2.1(b).

First, on the board draw the frame of the sketch and the top half of the sun, as shown in Figure 2.1(a). Have the class copy this into their notebooks or onto a separate sheet of paper. Tell them that the complete picture will show a house in a landscape. They have to ask you questions to find out the missing details, for example:

Where exactly is the house?
What kind of roof does it have?
Where is the front door?
How many windows are there on the second
   floor of the house?
What's on the right of the house?
What does the tree on the far right look like?
Which way is the smoke blowing?

They can also ask *Yes/No* questions, if appropriate:

Is the sun directly above the house?
Is the tree on the right a pine tree?

Answer each question briefly but clearly, and make sure everyone draws each new detail.

15

Encourage the quieter students, as well as the more confident ones, to ask questions. At the end of the session everyone should have a sketch similar to the one in Figure 2.1(b).

2.2   What did you say?

Warm-up *(1–2 minutes)*

Books are closed. Explain to the class that you're going to tell them a story. If they don't understand something you said, they should stop you and use a *Wh-* question to find out what they missed. For example, tell the following story, but when you get to a word in parentheses, mumble (you can say "er-er-er" instead of saying the word clearly). Begin like this:

Yesterday I went to the (laundromat) *to wash some clothes.*

A student then asks: "Where *did you go?*" and you answer: "To the laundromat." Continue the story as follows:

When I got there, I discovered that I'd forgotten to bring some (soap). *So I called* (my friend) *and asked her to bring it for me. But she couldn't do it because* (she was baking cookies). *Then I decided to* (buy some soap from the machine). *But it cost* (2 dollars), *and I only had one dollar. At that point I felt* (very frustrated). *So I took my clothes and went over to my friend's house and ate some* (cookies).

Procedure

A   Books are open. Begin by explaining the situation. Get started by forming the first two questions for part A as a class. Then have everyone write the remaining questions individually. Alternatively, divide the class into pairs to complete the exercise.

While students are doing this activity, go around checking, pointing out errors as necessary.

SAMPLE ANSWERS
Where are you going next month?
Who did you write to?*
When do you have to be back home?
How much does the ticket cost?
Who said she'd meet you at the airport?
Where would you like to go (while you're there)?
Why have you always wanted to go there?
How many seats are still left?
When does the flight leave?
When is the return flight?
Who / What could I bring with me?

* *Whom did you write to?* and *To whom did you write?* are also possible here, but they are generally considered too formal to be used in a conversation between friends.

B   This is the same type of activity as part A, but here the sentences are generated by the students about real events. Demonstrate what is required by writing these sentences on the board:

I left home at 8:30 in the morning.
I had a cup of coffee later in the morning.
I had lunch at 12:30 yesterday.

Then erase the words as shown below. Ask the class to say what questions they'd have to ask to find out the missing information.

I left home at   in the morning.
   When (What time) did you leave home?
I had   later in the morning.
   What did you have later in the morning?
I   at 12:30 yesterday.
   What did you do at 12:30?

Students without pencils or erasers can write in pen and "blacken out" the one piece of information.

C   *Pair work*   Each person looks at the other's sentences and asks questions to find out what has been erased.

Follow-up

Ask the class to "interview" you about your most recent vacation. Or they could interview each other, if you prefer. Some questions they might ask are:

When did you go on vacation?
Where did you go for your vacation?
What did you enjoy most about your vacation?
Where did you stay?

2.3   I'd like to ask you . . .

Warm-up *(2–3 minutes)*

Demonstrate the use of indirect questions by politely asking members of the class some personal questions. For example:

I'd like to ask where you were born.
Could you tell me what your phone number is?
Would you mind telling me how many brothers and sisters you have?

Use some direct questions, too, so that students can see the difference:

Where were you born?
What is your phone number?
How many brothers and sisters do you have?

Procedure

A   The purpose of this activity is to remind students that we can show *politeness* and *respect* by using indirect questions. In the situation illustrated on page 5 of the Student's Book, the interviewer is young and inexperienced. She's talking to a famous person who is older and commands her respect. Explain to students that one is *always* polite, but sometimes we show *extra* politeness to people who are older, in a position of authority, or strangers to us. (In case the question comes up, it should be clear that the reason for extra politeness is *not* because of gender.)

First, elicit two or three sample questions from the class. Then have students work in pairs and write down five more questions. Move around the class, offering suggestions and advice. Discuss relevant errors before you move on to part B. The change in word order from

direct to indirect questions is likely to cause difficulties.

Some other questions the young reporter might be asking are:

I'd like to ask you what your most memorable experience has been.
Could you tell me how long you have lived here?
Would you mind telling me when you stopped working?
Could you tell me how many grandchildren you have?

B   Allow the "reporters" time to prepare their lines of questioning - but they shouldn't write down the exact words of the questions. The "reporters" could work together as one large group to do this, while the "famous people" decide who they are going to be and think about the kinds of information they may be asked to give.

Note that once the interview is under way, the indirect forms are normally only used when we want to be extra polite or tactful (especially with sensitive questions). Otherwise "regular" direct question forms are used.

Listen carefully to the pairs at work and note any relevant errors that you should point out later. Allow time for questions from the class at the end.

Follow-up

Have the members of each pair change roles so that the "famous people" become "reporters" and have a chance to ask the questions.

2.4   Where were you . . . ?

Warm-up *(1–2 minutes)*

Look at the dialogue in part A. Ask the class to suggest *why* the detective is asking the suspect (the person who you think has done something wrong) these questions (e.g., he thinks the suspect robbed someone, committed a crime, etc.). Tell them that the crime was committed some time between 10:30 p.m. and midnight near the movie theater. Then do the procedure.

Procedure

A   Students should write the detective's questions, either as homework or in class. The following answers are suggestions only, and several variations are possible.

SAMPLE ANSWERS
What **was the name of the movie?** OR What **movie did you see?**
When **did the movie end / finish?** OR When **was it over?**
Who **did you go with?**
Where **did you go then / after the movie / afterwards?**
What **time did you get / arrive home?**

B   Some more questions the detective might ask are:

What happened in the movie? Tell me the story.
Who were the stars of the movie?
How long did the movie last?
Where exactly were you at 11:30?
What did you do when you got home?
What time did you go to bed?
When did you fall asleep?
When did you wake up the next morning?

Follow-up

Have the class role-play the interrogation. Encourage the suspects to make up their own answers. Or have students interrogate you as a "suspect."

3 The past: What happened?
The present perfect: What has happened?

Grammar summary

Practice in forming and using the simple past and present perfect to ask questions and make statements about past events and experiences.

Using the simple past:

I went *to Brazil* **in 1990.**
I enjoyed *my visit to Rio* **in June.**
I didn't get up *until 9 o'clock* **yesterday morning.**

Using the present perfect:

Have *you* **ever been** *to Japan?*
I've never been *to Thailand.*
Have *you* **written** *those letters* **yet?**
I've already written *the letters.***

*Students may hear sentences like these used in informal conversation:
I already ate lunch. instead of *I've already eaten lunch.*
Did you eat yet? instead of *Have you eaten yet?*

Forming and using the simple past and present perfect forms of common irregular verbs and some regular verbs that can cause difficulties:

go – went – gone
choose – chose – chosen
leave – left – left
lay – laid – laid
lie — lay – lain
lie – lied – lied
I'd like to **see** *the Amazon.*
I **saw** *the Nile last year.*
I've never **seen** *the Mississippi.*

Relevant errors

✗ I've been there yesterday.
✗ Have you ever went to Hawaii?
✗ I goed there last summer.
✗ It were beautiful there.
✗ What did Einstein?
✗ She's been born in 1975.
✗ He lied on the floor.
✗ He laid on the floor.
✗ She was dropping the vase on the floor.

3.1 Communication activity: Have you ever . . . ?

Warm-up (*3–4 minutes*)

Books are closed. Ask the class some questions about places they have visited, and about places in the country or region they're studying in. For example, if your class were taking place in Florida, you might ask:

Have any of you been to Sea World? What was it like? What did you see there?
Has anyone been to Walt Disney World? What was it like? What did you enjoy about it? Did you visit Epcot Center?
Have you been to the Kennedy Space Center? What was it like? What did you do there?
Have you been to Fort Myers? Did you visit Thomas Edison's winter home?

Make sure the follow-up questions are answered accurately, using the simple past. Call on members of the class to correct errors.

Books are open. Ask students to study the sample dialogue before they begin the communication activity. Draw their attention to the verb forms used in the dialogue.

The present perfect tense (with *ever*) is used here to ask about events that may have happened *some* time in the past – the person asking the question doesn't have any specific time in mind. Once the other speaker identifies a specific time in the past, both speakers use the present tense.

Procedure

Pair work   Divide the class into pairs. Student A should look at Activity 3, while Student B looks at Activity 9. If there's an odd number of students in your class, a third student can join forces with Student A and share the information. (Unless otherwise stated, all the communication activities will generally work in a group of 3, with two students sharing the same information and working as a "team.")

Make sure everyone reads the instructions in Activity 3 or 9 carefully before beginning. If necessary, explain the instructions in your own words, making it clear that students should take turns asking the questions, not just "interviewing" or "being interviewed." Point out that it's possible to make the activity more entertaining by inventing some experiences – but let your students decide whether they want to do this, as some people may feel uncomfortable.

Listen carefully as you go from pair to pair, and make notes of the relevant errors you overhear. This activity can be treated as a "diagnosis," to find out which aspects of your students' use of past verb forms need to be improved.

When most of the questions in the activities have been covered, tell the class about the relevant errors you noted, and call on them to suggest corrections.

Follow-up

1. Each student reports to the class something interesting about her or his partner. The speaker should use the simple past to refer to a definite time, for example: "My partner ate lobster last summer, but while he was eating, he discovered the lobster was still alive!"

2. This whole-class activity is for students who find it difficult to "switch" from using the present perfect (*Have you ever . . . ?* / *Yes, I have*) to simple past (*I rode one last summer* / *I fell off*) in conversations like the one in 3.1.

Find out if anyone in the class has:

-   flown in a 747, in another kind of airplane, in a helicopter, or in a small plane
-   eaten oysters, pecan pie, papaya, or mango
-   swum in the Atlantic, in the Pacific, in a lake, or in a river
-   been to Asia, to South America, to North America, to Europe
-   seen the latest video or movie that's playing

Follow this pattern as you ask the questions; members of the class answer them:

Teacher: *Has anyone ever flown in a 747?*
Student: *Yes, I have!*
Teacher: *Tell us about it.*
Student: *Well, it was a very comfortable flight. I went from here to New York to visit my relatives. I had a good time while I was there.*
Teacher: *Great, thanks! Has anyone else flown in a 747?*

If you know your class well, you'll be able to add to these ideas to include everyone's experiences!

3.2   Go – went – gone

Warm-up *(2–3 minutes)*

Books are closed. Write *go – went – gone* on the board. Ask the class to explain what these words are and how they differ. Have students use each word in some sentences, and write them on the board. For example:

I go to the store every day.
Yesterday I went to the store.
I haven't gone to the store yet today.

Then ask the class to name the three forms of as many other verbs as they can think of quickly.

Procedure

Books are open. Before starting the pair work, elicit from students how the first two or three blanks should be filled in. Make sure they understand the meanings of the verbs in the lists, and elicit sentences using any verbs that have meanings they are unsure of.

The incomplete table includes some of the "problem verbs" that intermediate students often find difficult or get confused.

A *Pair work*   Working together will help students feel more confident than working alone. Be prepared for puzzled questions, especially about the second column, but encourage everyone to try and work things out as far as possible.

Go through the correct answers with the class.

ANSWERS

Base form	Past tense	Past participle
beat	beat	**beaten**
bite	**bit**	bitten
blow	**blew**	blown
catch	caught	**caught**
choose	**chose**	**chosen**
drive	**drove**	**driven**
eat	**ate**	**eaten**
fall	fell	**fallen**
feel	felt	**felt**
fly	**flew**	flown
hide	hid	**hidden**
hold	**held**	held
lay[1]	**laid**	**laid**
lie[2]	lay	**lain**
lie[3]	lied	**lied**
lead	led	**led**
leave	left	**left**
live	**lived**	**lived**
lose	**lost**	**lost**
rise	rose	**risen**
steal	**stole**	**stolen**

[1]lay = place something
[2]lie = recline (as on a sofa)
[3]lie = tell untruths

Base form	Past tense	Past participle
tear	**tore**	torn
throw	**threw**	thrown
wear	**wore**	**worn**

B   Ask everyone to pick ten of the "most difficult" verbs from the list in part A (i.e., the ones they had to puzzle over most), and write sentences using them. First, look at the examples together. This can be done in class, working in pairs or groups of three, or as homework. (If this quantity of sentences seems too large, specify a smaller number.)

Finally, ask the class to suggest other verbs that they find hard to remember or get confused about. Discuss these with the class. Write them on the board and have the class copy them into their notebooks, to help them remember.

Follow-up

In this pair work activity, students find out about the previous years of each other's life, starting with last year, then the year before that, and so on, back in time. They make some use of the past continuous, which is a focus of the following unit, and continue to practice the simple past.

1. Write the last 20 years or so on the board in reverse order (1992, 1991, 1990, etc.) and explain how this activity works.
2. Write this model conversation on the board:

Where were you living in 1991?
– I was living in . . .
And what happened to you in that year / when you were there?
– I moved to a new apartment and I got a new job. What about you?

Have the class ask you questions about the previous years of your life, following the same pattern.
3. Arrange the class in pairs to ask and answer questions. Some students may prefer to pick out just the most memorable years of their lives, rather than talk about every year.
4. Now rearrange the pairs so that everyone has someone *different* to talk to. This can be done

simply by having students turn the other way, so that the people who were talking to the person on their left talk to the person on their right and vice versa. Now they tell their new partner about their first partner's life, starting at the *beginning* this time.

3.3   Have you done that yet?

Warm-up *(3–4 minutes)*

Books are closed. Write the words *already* and *yet* on the board. Have the class suggest some sentences in which these words can be used (with the present perfect) and write them on the board. For example:

Have *you* **had** *lunch yet?*
I've already **finished** *this work.*
We **haven't** *started the pair work yet.*
We've *already* **done** *Unit 2.*

Procedure

Ask students if they, or people they know, ever make lists. Find out why and when they make lists and what kinds of things they put on their lists. Then show the class a list you have made titled "Things to Do Today" and simply read them the items on it. (You might wish to include a few humorous items, such as "take a nap before dinner, take a nap after dinner, make up a very hard English test.") Finally, refer students to Tony's list in the Student's Book.

A   *Pair work*   Make sure everyone realizes that the unchecked items in Tony's list are the things that have *not* yet been done.

SAMPLE ANSWERS
He's already arranged to meet Sandy for dinner. He hasn't made dinner reservations yet.
He's already done yesterday's homework. But he hasn't done today's homework yet.
He hasn't washed the car yet. He's already filled the car with gas.

He hasn't written to his parents yet. He's already bought a birthday card for his mom.
He's already read today's newspaper. But he hasn't watched the news on TV yet.

B   *Pair work*   To help students think of some things they might have done today, have everyone make a list of things they normally do each day. They can add to the list any particular things on *today's* agenda. Use your own list to run through the exercise with the whole class. Then have everyone start talking in pairs.

Follow-up

A   Have students write sentences about two things they have *never* done, two things they have done *lots of times,* and two things they haven't done *yet* in their lives. For example:

I've never visited Spain, but I've always wanted to.
I've played soccer lots of times.
I haven't gotten married yet, but I guess I will someday.

B   Have students, working in pairs, make up more sentences like the following:

I've never been to Japan, but I've eaten sushi.
I've never played soccer, but I've seen lots of soccer matches on TV.
I've never visited Brazil, but I've heard a lot about the Carnival there.

3.4   Communication activity: Famous people

Warm-up *(5 minutes)*

Books are closed. Ask the class to give you the names of some famous people from their own countries. Write their names on the board and ask the class if they can tell you when each person was born and, if they're dead, when they died.

In case your students don't know the birth or death dates of any famous people, you may need to be prepared to list three or four famous people from your students' countries on the board, together with the years of their births (and deaths). Then have students form sentences from that information.

Procedure

Pair work   Student A looks at Activity 2 and Student B at Activity 15. (A third student can share A's information if necessary.) Each student has a list about some famous people of the past. The two lists put together give the complete, correct set of names and dates.

Don't worry if some of the names are unfamiliar to some of your students. Encourage them to find out from their partners about the people they don't know about.

Here, for your information and to help sort out any disagreements among the students, is some information about the people listed in Activities 2 and 15.

Ludwig van Beethoven (1770–1872): German composer and pianist who wrote magnificent music in spite of losing his hearing; famous compositions include the "Moonlight Sonata" and the Fifth and Ninth Symphonies

Queen Victoria (1819–1901): Queen of England from 1837 to 1901

Susan Brownell Anthony (1820–1906): American leader of "votes for women" movement

Marie Curie (1867–1934): Polish-born scientist; studied radioactivity; awarded Nobel Prizes for physics (1903) and chemistry (1911)

Mata Hari (1876–1917): Dutch-born; had a successful dance career in Paris when she became a spy for Germany in World War I; arrested by the French for espionage and executed by a firing squad

Albert Einstein (1879–1955): German-born American physicist; developed theory of relativity; awarded Nobel Prize in 1921 for work on photoelectricity

Amelia Earhart (1897–1937): American aviator; first woman to fly across the Atlantic; disappeared on attempt to fly around the world

Eleanor Roosevelt (1884–1962): American reformer, politician, and diplomat; wife of American President Franklin D. Roosevelt

Charlie Chaplin (1889–1977): British-born American comedian and movie star of such films as *The Tramp, City Lights,* and *Modern Times*

Marilyn Monroe (1926–1962): American movie star; famous films include *Some Like It Hot, Bus Stop,* and *The Misfits*

James Dean (1931–1955): American movie star famous for his roles in *Rebel without a Cause, East of Eden,* and *Giant*

Elvis Presley (1926–1977): American rock 'n' roll singer and guitar player whose famous songs included "Heartbreak Hotel," "Blue Suede Shoes," and "All Shook Up"; also starred in movies, such as *Love Me Tender*

Follow-up

Ask the class to tell you more about the famous people they named for the warm-up. What were they most famous for? What did they do?

3.5   One fine day . . .

Warm-up *(3–5 minutes)*

Look at the cartoons in the Student's Book with the class and, without discussing the story line or sequence of events, deal with any questions on vocabulary.

Procedure

A   *Group work*   Divide the class into groups of about 4. There are several possible "correct" arrangements of the pictures in the cartoon strip – don't imply that one is "best."

B   *Pair work*   Rearrange the class into pairs, consisting of members of different groups.

Figure 3.1

Each person tells her or his version of the story to the other.

C   Writing the story may take up too much time in class, so it can be assigned as homework.

Before the written work is handed in to you, have everyone read another student's work and comment on it. Students can learn from each other in this way, and the kind of feedback they give each other is usually very motivating.

When marking the work, distinguish between relevant errors and other errors (see page 5).

SAMPLE ANSWER
(Figure 3.1 shows the cartoon numbered to correspond with the following story.)

One day a woman was walking home from the supermarket when she saw a bundle of money on the sidewalk. She took the money and rushed home to show it to her husband. They started thinking about what they would do with all that money. She wanted to buy a sportscar. He wanted to take a long vacation at a beach resort.

Suddenly a police officer knocked at their door. The officer said that the money had been stolen from a bank. The officer took the money from the woman, who didn't want to give it back. The next day, however, the woman was in a good mood again. She and her husband got a $10,000 reward for returning the missing money!

Follow-up

This game gives extra practice in asking and answering questions about past experiences. This activity can be done by students working in groups of 4 or 5, or if you have a small class, it can be done as a whole-class activity.

1. Prepare a slip of paper for each member of the class. Write *False* on enough slips for one member of each group to get one, and write *Truth* on all the rest. (VARIATION: Have a random number of "false" slips in each group, not just one.)
2. Distribute the slips, making sure one and only one member of each group gets a "false" slip. Don't let students peek, and don't tell them how many "liars" there are in each group.
3. Explain the idea of the game: Everyone has to tell a story about her or his past – a good theme is "A Vacation I Remember." The false

24

stories will be fictitious and the others will be true.

4. Allow a few minutes for students to think of and prepare their stories, making notes if necessary.

5. Each member of the group tells her or his story. The others should ask questions to test the veracity of the story.

6. Students have to decide who was telling the truth and who wasn't, and explain how they made their decision.

7. The "liars" identify themselves.

4

The past continuous: What was happening?
The present perfect continuous:
What has been happening?

Grammar summary

Using the past continuous to ask questions and make statements about simultaneous activities:

He **was watching** *TV while you* **were reading.**
What **were** *you* **doing** *while I* **was waiting** *for you?*

Using the past continuous to describe actions that began before a point in time and continued after:

What **were** *you* **doing** *at 9 o'clock this morning?*
I **was driving** *to work at 8:45.*

Using the past continuous to describe interrupted actions:

I **was cooking** *dinner when the telephone rang.*

The present perfect continuous describes events that started in the past and are still happening (especially with *since* and *for* and after *How long . . .* questions):

How long **have you been studying** *English?*
I **have been living** *here for five years.* (*five years* is a period of time)
I've **been waiting** *here* since *six o'clock.* (*six o'clock* is a point in time)

Different meanings of the simple past, past continuous, and past perfect:

I **got** *out of bed when the alarm clock went off.*
(I got out of bed immediately after the alarm went off.)
I **was getting** *out of bed when the alarm clock went off.* (I started to get out of bed when it went off.)

I **had** *already* **gotten** *out of bed when the alarm clock went off.* (I got out of bed. Then the alarm went off.)

Relevant errors

✗ He was having three cups of coffee when I arrived.
✗ I was recognizing him but not remembering his name.
✗ We were hearing a crash while he washed the dishes.
✗ There was a thunderstorm while our tennis game.
✗ It happened during we were playing tennis.
✗ I've been studying English since five years.
✗ How long are you studying English?

4.1   What were you doing?

Warm-up *(3–5 minutes)*

Books are closed. Write an earlier time today, such as 8:45, on the board. Ask everyone to think back to what they were doing at that time. Write another time, such as "ten minutes before this class started," and give a few moments for reflection. Then ask students to tell you what they were doing at various times earlier today. For example:

What were you doing at 8:45 this morning?
What were you doing ten minutes before this class started?

Procedure

A   Books are open. Working with the whole class, ask students to suggest what answers they think the man in the cartoon gave. For example:

I was watching my favorite show on TV when you called.
I turned it off when you called.
I missed the end of the show. / I didn't see the rest of the show.

B   First students work in pairs to work out the different meanings together. Then discuss the different meanings with the whole class.

ANSWERS
She was having dinner when her husband came home.   **She was in the middle of eating her dinner when he came home.**
She had dinner when her husband came home.   **She started eating dinner shortly after he returned.**
She had already had dinner when her husband came home.   **She was finished with dinner before he returned.**

He went to the store when the sun came out.   **He waited until the sun started to shine. Then he went to the store.**
He was going to the store when the sun came out.   **He was on his way to the store when the sun started to shine.**
He had already been to the store when the sun came out.   **He returned from the store. Then the sun started to shine.**

Ask students to make up more examples of sentences that contrast the tenses.

C   There are many different ways of filling in the blanks. Encourage the class to use their own ideas. Students who have trouble with this should work in pairs. Students who finish early can try to think of more than one answer for each blank.

Have everyone tell you what she or he has written. Discuss with the class what is or is not correct and the differences in meaning.

Encourage questions about the different meanings implied by different verb forms.

SAMPLE ANSWERS
1. We **were sitting / had just had tea** on the patio when it started to rain.
2. They **were driving** along slowly when a deer ran across the road.
3. She **was reaching / (had) just reached the most interesting part of** the book when she fell asleep.
4. He **was opening / opened** the letter when his wife came into the room.
5. I **was drinking / making myself** some coffee when the lights went out.
6. She **was looking / was staring out of** the window when the phone rang.

A more advanced class should be reminded that there are a number of verbs that are not usually used with the continuous form of the verb. These include verbs such as:

taste, hear, smell, etc.
like, hate, love, etc.
believe, imagine, know, etc.
recognize, remember, etc.
belong to, contain, etc.
seem, appear, etc.

These verbs are sometimes called "stative" verbs, because they express a physical or mental state.

Follow-up

This activity practices using the past continuous when talking about actions that were taking place at a particular, exact time (e.g., *At 8:23 this morning I was eating my breakfast.*).

1. Write this "framework" on the board:

Yesterday I got up at ....
I started breakfast at............ and finished at
....
I left home at .... , went to .... , and arrived there at ....
At............ in the morning I ....
I started lunch at............ and finished at
....

At............ in the afternoon I ....
I arrived home again at............ and had dinner
  at ....
At............ in the evening I ....
I went to bed at............ and fell asleep at

  ....

2. Then, tell everyone what time you did the
first few things shown in the framework and
write these times in the blanks. For example:

*Yesterday I got up at 7:15. I started breakfast
at 7:50 and finished at 8:05. I left home at
8:23, went to work, and arrived there at
8:55 . . .*

Have the class ask you what you were doing at
specific times "in between" the given times. For
example:

Student 1: *What were you doing at 7:30?*
Teacher: *I was getting dressed / taking a
            shower.*
Student 2: *What were you doing at 7:59?*
Teacher: *I was eating breakfast and reading
            the newspaper.*
Student 3: *What were you doing at 8:19?*
Teacher: *I was looking for my car keys.*

Write a few more times in the blanks of the
framework and elicit more questions. Continue
in this way until the end of the framework.
3. Form pairs (or groups of 3). Each student
has to find out what the other was doing at
various times yesterday. For example:

Student 1: *What were you doing at 7:30?*
Student 2: *I was still asleep. What about you?*
Student 1: *Oh, I got up and had breakfast at
            7:25.*
Student 2: *I was still lying in bed then. I didn't
            get up till after 8.*

  If the class needs guidance, write a list of
times on the board to prompt questions. Also, a
pattern such as this may help:

What were you doing yesterday?
  .... *What about you?*
Oh, ...

  ....

To close the practice session, call on several
pairs to "perform" one of their conversations for
the whole class.

4.2   When the phone rang . . .

Warm-up *(3–10 minutes)*

Books are closed. Ask students: "What happens
when the phone rings where you live? Who
answers it? Is it ever difficult or annoying to
answer the phone? Why?"
  Tell and/or elicit a story or two about a time
when answering the phone was troublesome or
funny. Then write on the board, *"When the
phone rang, I . . ."* Encourage students to
suggest a variety of imaginative responses, in
more than one verb tense if possible.

Procedure

Books are open. Begin by asking everyone to
suggest alternative ways of completing the
example. For instance:

*When the doorbell rang, I was at home having a
  snack and looking at the TV guide.*

This exercise can be done by students working
together in pairs. Or it can be done by students
working alone to write the sentences, and then
working in pairs to compare answers.

SAMPLE ANSWERS
2. When the lights went out, **he was sitting in
    his favorite armchair reading a book.**
3. When my alarm clock went off, **I was
    sleeping peacefully in my bed dreaming about
    my last summer vacation.**
4. When my guests arrived, **I was in the kitchen
    fixing dinner.**
5. When I met my old friend, **I was strolling in
    the park looking at the beautiful spring
    flowers.**
6. When the rain started, **we were sitting on the
    beach having a picnic.**

7. When they called me for the meeting, **I was sitting at my desk working on a report.**
8. When the phone rang, **I was looking out of the window admiring the view of the mountains.**

NOTE: *When . . .* clauses at the beginning of a sentence are often separated from the main clause by a comma: *When I've finished my work, I'll give you a call.* But it is also acceptable not to use a comma, especially in short sentences: *When I've finished I'll call you.*

Follow-up

1. Have students make up some more *when . . .* clauses. Write them on the board. Then see who can come up with the most creative completions. For example:

When I woke up this morning, . . .
– *it was pouring rain while the sun was shining.*
– *two large black birds were sitting on my bed, looking at me.*

2. *When . . .* clauses often *follow* the main clause. For example: *I was sitting at home watching TV when the doorbell rang.* In pairs or as a class, have students practice the sentences in Exercise 4.2 with the *when . . .* clause after the main clause.

4.3   How long have you been . . . ?

Procedure

Start by looking at the dialogue with the class. Ask students how they would feel if they were the people in the picture. Have they had a similar experience?

Make sure everyone understands that *for* is used with periods of time and *since* is used with points in time. Have students suggest some time phrases that would be used with *for* and with *since*. For example:

for

   10 minutes, a long time, 2 weeks, 3 years, my whole life, etc.

since

   8 o'clock, 1989, the beginning of the week, I was a child, last summer, etc.

A   This exercise shows that *for* and *since* are used to relate past time to the time *now*. This is why it is important first for students to fill in today's day and date (e.g., *Tuesday, July 7*) and the time now (e.g., *7:45 p.m.*). Only then can they fill in the blanks in the sentences, by working out the difference between the time now and the time indicated in the sentence.

SAMPLE ANSWERS
These answers assume the following date and time.
   Today's date **Tuesday, 7 July 1992**
   Time now **7:45 p.m.**

2. Bill started English classes five years ago, so he**'s been studying English** since **1987.**
3. Peter first moved into his apartment four years ago. That means he **has been living there** since **1988.**
4. Maria passed her driving test in January, so she **has been driving** for **six** months.
5. Ed began work in this company two months ago, so he **has been working here** since **May.**
6. It started raining at about 9 a.m., so it **has been raining** for **over ten** hours.
7. We all sat down at the beginning of the class, so we **have been sitting here** for **20** minutes.   (Depending on when the lesson started)
8. They started work on the project on Sunday, so now they **have been working on it** for **two** days.

B   Students begin this part on their own by writing down five questions beginning with *"How long have you been . . . ?"* For example:

How long have you been living at your present address?
How long have you been studying English?
How long have you been sitting in this room?

How long have you been working with
  Communicative Grammar Practice?

Put the following pattern on the board:

A: *How long have you* .... *?*
B: *Oh, let me think* .... *I* (past tense) ....
  ago.
A: *So that means you've* .... *since*
  .... *.*
B: *Right.*   OR   *No, since* .... *.*

Demonstrate how to use the pattern by having
some students ask you a few of their questions.
Then put students in pairs to ask each other
their questions, following the pattern.

Follow-up

Have everyone write down the beginnings of six
more sentences using *for* or *since*. Then they
hand the sentences to a partner, who has to
complete them in a suitable way. For example:

We've been waiting for . . .
– half an hour.
The weather has been fine since . . .
– the middle of last week.

Or, instead of having students exchange
papers, you could collect the papers and either
(1) dictate several of the sentence beginnings to
the class to write down and complete, or (2)
copy some of the sentence beginnings on a
handout to make a homework exercise written
by the students themselves.

4.4   I looked out the window . . .

Warm-up *(1–2 minutes)*

Books are closed. Ask students to tell you
something they saw when they looked out the
window at home, work, or school yesterday, last
night, or this morning. Tell them what you saw
from one of your windows, to get them started.
For example:

I saw my neighbor painting her house.
I saw a bird building a nest.

Procedure

Books are open. Start by looking at the
illustration with the class. Ask them to identify
all the activities that were going on. Or, to add a
bit of drama, play a "memory" game. Give the
class one minute to study the picture and then
have them close their books. Ask them to
identify the activities they remember. Put a
check on the board for each activity
remembered. Then open the books and see how
many activities the students remembered
correctly.

The paragraphs can be written at home or, if
there's time, in class. Before they are handed in
to you, have everyone read another student's
work and comment on it.

5 | *Past, present, and future*

Grammar summary

Practice in using the present perfect, present continuous, and *going to* to talk about recent events, current events, and future events:

She **has had** *lunch.*   (recent past)
   *She***'s had** *lunch.*
She **is having** *lunch.*   (now)
   *She***'s having** *lunch.*
She **is going to have** *lunch.*   (soon)
   *She***'s going to have** *lunch.*

Using the simple past and *used to* to talk about past activities and habits:

There was a time when I **smoked** *50 cigarettes a day.*   (a long time ago)
I **used to be** *a heavy smoker.*   (but not anymore)
Did *you* **use to play** *volleyball?*   (some time in the past)

Using the simple present to talk about current habits:

I **don't smoke** *anymore.*
I only **watch** *volleyball now.*

Using *for* and *since* with the present perfect:

I **haven't seen** *him* **since 1988.**   (point in time)
I **have been feeling** *sick* **for several days.**   (period of time)

Relevant errors

✗ What is happened?
✗ Don't you used to play volleyball?
✗ I didn't play golf since three years.
✗ I haven't seen him since three years.
✗ I have been reading six pages so far.
✗ She still didn't do it yet.
✗ I have stopped smoking five years ago.
✗ I am used to drink a lot of milk.

5.1   A woman alone

Warm-up *(1–2 minutes)*

Books are closed. Write *alone* on the board. Ask students: "Do you like to be alone? When do you like to be alone?"
   As part of the conversation, tell the class a situation in which you like to be alone.

Procedure

The painting is *Automat* (1927), by Edward Hopper. Before students start talking, get everyone to look at the picture in silence for a minute or so. This will encourage everyone to use her or his imagination.

Group work   Divide the class into groups of 3 or 4. Ask them to discuss the picture and decide together what has happened earlier – and what is going to happen next. For example:

She has had a fight with her boyfriend.
Her boyfriend hasn't shown up for a date.
She's lost her keys and can't get into her apartment.
She's just quit her job and is feeling bad about it.
She has just heard some bad news.

She's going to call him and tell him to meet her in the cafe.
She's going to wait until he arrives.
She's going to try to get a new job.
She's going to spend the evening in the cafe.

During the discussion, circulate around the class, making a note of the relevant errors you overhear.
   Have one person from each group tell the rest of the class what their group's theories are.

Point out the relevant errors you overheard earlier and ask everyone to suggest how they should be corrected.

Follow-up

Show the class some more pictures that allow for multiple interpretations (these could be mounted on cardboard and used again and again). Ask students to suggest what has just happened, describe what's happening now, and suggest what is going to happen later.

5.2   Communication activity: What's going on?

Procedure

Before starting this activity, remind students not to look at each other's picture, only at their own. Remind them of the purpose of this kind of "information gap" activity (see Communication Activities on page 6 and the warm-up for Exercise 1.4).

Pair work   Divide the class into pairs. Student A looks at Activity 20, and Student B at 31.

During the conversation, make sure everyone talks about the events *during, before,* and *after* each scene. At the end, ask for questions on vocabulary and point out the relevant errors you overheard. Have volunteers share their stories with the class.

SAMPLE ANSWERS
Student A (Activity 20, page 88 in the Student's Book)

Two couples are saying goodbye at a train station. The woman on the left is going back to college after a short break, and the other woman is going to visit a relative. The men are kissing them goodbye.

Earlier, the couple on the left went out for a romantic last meal together at a restaurant. They had a good time and laughed a lot. The other couple had a quiet dinner at home. The woman
packed her bags. She also phoned her relatives to say what time she was arriving.

After the train leaves, everyone will feel sad. The women and men will miss each other at first. But the student will sit next to a very handsome young man on the train. They'll talk and have a good time. The other woman will read a book on the train. The young man will go to a movie. The other man will return home and watch TV.

Student B (Activity 31, page 92 in the Student's Book)

A young couple are in an airport. A customs officer is checking their baggage. The couple are waiting patiently.

Earlier they had been on a ten-hour flight from California to Germany. The flight was long and boring. They watched two movies, which weren't very good. They ate breakfast and lunch on the plane as well. Every hour or so they got up and stretched and walked around.

Next they will go to their apartment. They'll take a shower and relax. They'll also unpack their bags. Then they'll phone some friends and invite them to come over. When their friends arrive, the couple will give them gifts that they bought on their vacation.

Follow-up

Ask everyone to bring some of her or his own photographs to class (vacation photos, family occasions, excursions, etc.).

Then, in groups of 3 or 4, students look at each other's photos and talk about what's going on – and ask each other what happened shortly before and shortly after each photo was taken.

5.3   What has happened?

Warm-up   (*2–3 minutes*)

Books are closed. Write these words on the board, one by one: *angry, very sad, frightened (afraid, scared), happy, depressed.* After you write each one, ask the class: "When do you feel this way?" Elicit one or two suggestions for each word.

Procedure

Books are open. Begin by asking the class to look at the face on the left and describe the man's expression. Ask them to suggest *various* things that have happened earlier, and *various* things that are going to happen later. For example:

He's angry and upset. Someone has just crashed into his car. He's going to have to pay for the damage.

Pair work   Divide the class into pairs or groups of 3. Each cartoon can be interpreted in several ways – encourage everyone to think of *various* things that have happened earlier and *various* things that are going to happen later. Ask pairs to write down their best ideas about each picture. Then have each pair share their ideas with another pair, or with the whole class.

SAMPLE ANSWERS

**She's very upset. She's failed an important test
    She's not going to tell her parents about this.
He's frightened. He's just seen a ghost. He's
    going to run away as fast as possible.
She's happy. She's just been promoted. She's
    going to go out and celebrate.
They're sad / depressed. They've just received
    some very bad news.
They're going to feel bad about it for a long time.**

5.4   Communication activity: Those were the days!

Warm-up *(2–3 minutes)*

Books are closed. On the board write: *I used to play baseball.* Ask students what this sentence means (something done in the past but not anymore). Then write this dialogue on the board:

Didn't you use to play baseball?
– Yes, I did.
Do you still play baseball?
– No, I don't play it anymore. Now I play golf.

Practice this dialogue with the class, substituting different sports (or other things, like musical instruments), if you like. Point out that the underlined words are stressed because they introduce new information.

Leave the pattern dialogue on the board so that students can refer to it if they need help during the communication activity.

Procedure

Books are open. Before dividing the class into pairs, have everyone read the examples in the illustration.

Pair work   Divide the class into pairs. Have partners imagine that they're two old friends who haven't seen each other for five years. Student A looks at Activity 35, and Student B at 48.

Tell students to find out what is *still* true about their partner, and to put a check mark next to those things. They can use the dialogue from the Warm-up if they need help getting started.

Walk around and listen to the conversations, noting relevant errors and problems with intonation. Discuss these at the end of the activity.

Follow-up

Divide the class into pairs or groups of 3 or 4. Ask students to think about their own lives and remember what their lives were like when they were several years younger: say, five or ten years ago. Encourage them to use *used to, don't anymore,* and *still do.*

5.5   Before TV

Warm-up *(2–3 minutes)*

Books are closed. Write *TV* on the board. Ask students when they watch TV and how much TV they watch. Tell them a little about your TV habits. Ask if anyone doesn't like to watch TV, and why.

Procedure

Books are open. Look at the photo in the Student's Book and help the class with any vocabulary questions. Then discuss the first question with the whole class: "What did people use to do before they had television?" (For example, *They used to sew / play games / read / listen to the radio / talk more,* etc.)

A *Group work*   Divide the class into groups of 4 or 5. Point out that the questions in the Student's Book are questions for discussion – there are no "right answers." Students may need to guess and use their imagination in this activity.

B *Group work*   Retain the same groups as in part A. Ask the class to suggest how the questions they asked in part A might need to be adapted for this discussion, and which

questions would be irrelevant. For example:

How did people use to travel before we had airplanes?
How did people spend their evenings before electric lights were invented?

If a group runs out of things to say about the inventions and discoveries listed, ask them to think of more inventions to add to the list, and discuss those too. For example: *fax machines, air conditioning, supermarkets, CD players,* etc. Finally, open up the discussion to the whole class by asking each group to report on the most interesting points they made.

C   This can be done as homework, but before leaving class, students should write a few notes about what they discussed in class.

Follow-up

Have students show their paragraphs to the people they worked with in part B and ask them for comments.

6 | *Quantity*

Grammar summary

Practice in using "countable" nouns:

> *car(s)*   *fact(s)*   *dollar(s)*   *person(s)*
> *people*   *woman / women*   *kid(s)*
> *child / children*   *hour(s)*   *bottle(s)*
> *slice(s)*   etc.

*How **many** cars can you see?*
*That **is an** interesting fact.*
Only a few *people can afford a Porsche.*
Not many *people own a Mercedes.*
*Premium gas costs **a few** cents **more** than*
   unleaded.

Using "uncountable" nouns:

> *traffic*   *information*   *work*   *time*
> *beer*   *advice*   *bread*   *money*   *news*
> etc.

*How **much** traffic is there on the road?*
*This **is** interesting information.*   (but: *This is*
   an *interesting **piece of** information.*)
*My parents give me **too much** advice.*   (but:
   *They gave me a good **piece** of advice.*)
*So **much** of the news is depressing this week.*
*They don't spend as **much** money as we do.*
(but not: *How **many** moneys do you have?*)

Using appropriate expressions to describe one
item of "uncountable" nouns:

> *a cup of coffee*   *a jar of honey*   *a sheet of*
> *paper*   *a block of time*   etc.

Using nouns that are either "countable" or
"uncountable," depending on their meaning:

*I'd like **a glass** of milk.*
*Windows are made of **glass.***
*I'm going to buy **a paper.** (= a newspaper)*
*I need **some paper.** (= to write on)*
Two beers *please.*
How much beer is *left in the bottle?*

How many times *do I need to remind you?*
How much time *do I have to do it?*

Relevant errors

✗ How many moneys do you have?
✗ Can you give me an information?
✗ I'd like some informations.
✗ I have many advices for you.
✗ So many of the news are depressing.
✗ There was so much people in the room.

6.1   Countable or uncountable?

Warm-up *(5–10 minutes)*

Books are closed. Write the framework from the
Student's Book on the board:

COUNTABLE: A............   one............
         two............s   several............s
         not many............s   fewer............s
UNCOUNTABLE: Not much............
         less............

Hold up various items and ask the class to
say what you are holding – for example, two
keys, several pencils, a stack of paper, a bowl of
fruit. Show how students can check whether the
noun is countable (it has a plural form) or
uncountable (it doesn't have a plural form) by
filling in the blanks of the framework. For
example:

COUNTABLE: A key   one key   two keys
         several keys   not many keys
         fewer keys
but not:
UNCOUNTABLE: Not much keys   less keys

Procedure

Books are open. Make sure students are familiar with the vocabulary in the exercise before starting. Then as a class, discuss the first row of words: *money, dollar, cash, advice, scenery, election.* Write them in the framework to show how to check whether each word is countable or uncountable.

Explain that this exercise is only a check. The only sure way to know whether a word is countable is to look it up in the dictionary.

A *Pair work*   Divide the class into pairs or groups of 3. Circulate around the class, helping students as needed.

ANSWERS

English **U**	*food* **U**	*furniture* **U**	*gas* **U**
health **U**	*honey* **U**	*job* **C**	*journey* **C**
language **C**	*magazine* **C**	*meal* **C**	
meat **U**	*news* **U**	*oil* **U**	*paint* **U**
pasta **U**	*progress* **U**	*rain* **U**	*rice* **U**
river **C**	*safety* **U**	*salt* **U**	*snow* **U**
storm **C**	*table* **C**	*travel* **U**	*trip* **C**
vocabulary **U**	*water* **U**	*weather* **U**	
wine **U**	*word* **C**	*work* **U**	

NOTE: Some of the "uncountable" nouns listed in the Student's Book can, in certain circumstances, be "countable," as these examples show:

Vegetarians don't eat meat.   (uncountable)
but: *Beef and lamb are red meats.*   (countable)
I'm going to put some gas in my car.
   (uncountable)
but: *Carbon monoxide is a poisonous gas.*
   (countable)
I've got some work to do.   (uncountable)
but: *She's studying the works of Shakespeare.*
   (countable)
Guernica is an impressive work of art.
   (countable)

B   Students could write their six sentences together in pairs, or they could work alone for a few moments, or they could do this for homework. Check the sentences and point out any errors you spot in them.

Follow-up

Ask the class to think of some more nouns. Write them all on the board. Then have the class say which of them are countable and which are uncountable.

Most of the nouns suggested will probably turn out to be countable. If so, ask the class to come up with an *equal* number of uncountable nouns.

Remind a more advanced class that some nouns can be either countable or uncountable, depending on their meaning. Write these words on the board and ask the class to provide examples showing the different meanings:

beer   time   wine   age   wood   cake
experience   paper   sound

For example:

I'd like some cake.   (uncountable)
*I'm going to bake a cake for my next door
   neighbor.*   (countable)

6.2   So much! So many!

Procedure

Books are closed. Write the first sentence from the exercise on the board: *They have...........
that everyone envies them.* Have the students figure out what the missing words might be.

Books are open. Make sure that all the words in parentheses are familiar to the class.

A   This exercise can be done in pairs or by students working alone. Circulate around the class while students are doing it, offering advice or suggestions. Go over the correct answers before they do part B.

ANSWERS
2. **so many suggestions / so much advice**
3. **so much information / so many facts**
4. **so many experiments / so much research**
5. **so much homework / so many exercises**
6. **so much luggage / so many bags**

7. **so many reports / so much news**
8. **so much information / so many articles**

B   This can be done by students together in pairs. Tell the class that there are many possible ways of completing the sentences, and encourage fast-working students to think of more than one. Have each pair compare their sentences with another pair when they've finished. Then ask the various pairs to read their responses to the whole class. Alternatively the exercise could be done as homework.

SAMPLE ANSWERS
1. During our vacation we had **so much** fun that **we forgot all about work / school.**
2. The students in this class have made **so much** progress that **they'll all pass the exam.**
3. I made **so many** mistakes on the test that **I'm sure I'll flunk it.**
4. There was **so much** traffic that **we couldn't get across the street.**
5. In English there seems to be **so much** vocabulary that **it's impossible to learn it all.**
6. And there seem to be **so many** exceptions to every grammar rule that **it takes forever to learn them all!**

Follow-up

Have students highlight or write down the pairs of words in part A that they found most difficult or confusing. For homework, have them write sentences using them.

With a more advanced class, ask everyone to suggest how the following sentences might continue.

1. Some examples of nouns that are (perhaps unexpectedly) "plural" in English:

The police are . . .
A number of us are . . .
The majority of us are . . .
A lot of us are . . .
A group of us are . . .

2. Some examples of nouns that are (perhaps unexpectedly) "singular" in English:

The news is . . .
Measles is . . .

Politics is . . .
The new TV series has . . .
The United States is . . .
Economics is . . .

6.3   Communication activity: How much? How many?

Warm-up *(1–3 minutes)*

If possible, bring to class a few items or pictures of items in various containers: for example, a pack of gum, a packet (individual serving size) of sugar / salt, a carton of milk (empty!), a bar of candy. Ask students to identify the items. Then ask the class some questions, such as:

How many sticks are in a pack of gum?
How many packets of sugar do you think come in a package?
How many different containers can you buy milk in?   (carton, can, bottle, powdered milk in packets, etc.)

Procedure

This exercise practices expressing a quantity using uncountable nouns. Before students start part A, go through the first few examples with the class and ask them to suggest the correct answers. Explain any unfamiliar vocabulary in the lists.

A   *Pair work*   Divide the class into pairs or groups of 3 for this exercise.

Discuss the answers with the class before going on to part B. Note that we can also talk about *a spoonful of sugar, a can of beer, a carton of cigarettes,* and so on. Moreover, some of the usual containers the items come in may vary from country to country – some countries commonly use *cans* of milk, rather than *cartons,* for example.

SUGGESTED ANSWERS

1. a bar of   **2** beer
2. a bottle of   **6** bread

37

3. a box of   __8__ cake
4. a cube of   __1__ soap
5. a jar of   __3__ candy
6. a loaf of   __7__ cigarettes
7. a pack of   __5__ honey
8. a slice of   __4__ ice
9. a box of   __10__ soda
10. a can of   __9__ matches
11. a packet of   __13__ milk
12. a pot of   __15__ paper
13. a carton of   __11__ sugar
14. a pitcher of   __12__ tea
15. a sheet of   __16__ toothpaste
16. a tube of   __14__ water

B   *Pair work*   Before students refer to
their books, write *camping* on the board and ask
a few questions, such as "Who has been
camping? Who would like to go? Where do
(would) you like to camp? What do you need
for a camping trip?" Then have students
imagine they are on a camping trip with their
partner.

Student A looks at Activity 8 while Student B
looks at 39. Each student has a different list of
"things they have run out of," and "things they
still have left," some of which are countable and
some uncountable. The idea is to find out what
supplies their partner still has left, and say
what they have left.

This pattern for the conversation is given in
both activities:

A: *Do you have any* .... *left?*
B: *Yes. How much would you like?* OR *How
   many* .... *would you like?*
A: *(Number and containers),
   please.* OR *(Number), please.*
B: *I'm sorry, I only have* .... OR *Here you
   are!* (Students should accompany this by a
   "handing" gesture.)

Give students a minute to read the information
in their activity before starting. If the class is
not sure how to begin, demonstrate the exercise
by prompting a pair of students to ask and

answer back and forth while the rest of the class
watches.

Follow-up

This might be a good time to review irregular
plurals. Dictate these nouns and have the class
write down the plurals:

| *child* | *mouse* | *foot* | *tooth* | *goose* |
| *sheep* | *aircraft* | *fish* | *deer* | |

ANSWERS
| *children* | *mice* | *feet* | *teeth* | *geese* |
| *sheep* | *aircraft* | *fish* | *deer* | |

6.4   Spot the errors

Warm-up *(2–4 minutes)*

Books are closed. Tell the class: "We're going to
do something crazy for a minute. Please give me
example sentences that are *wrong* – example
sentences that you know have errors with
countable or uncountable nouns."

Elicit two or three sentences and write them
on the board. As suggestions are given, thank
the students enthusiastically for the "wrong"
sentences and ask them: "Are you *sure* it's
wrong? I need incorrect sentences – sentences
with errors about countable and uncountable
nouns." (Students often enjoy the novelty of
being *asked* to commit errors.)

Then, with the class's help, underline the
mistake(s) in each sentence and write the
corrections above the incorrect words.

Procedure

Books are open. Explain that the sentences in
the exercise contain common mistakes. Ask the
class to tell you what's wrong with the first
sentence. Have them underline the error and
write in the correction.

Pair work   First the pairs find the mistake(s) in each sentence and underline them. Then they write the corrections.

At the end, go over the sentences with the class and make sure they're aware of *every* mistake in the sentences.

ANSWERS
(Mistakes are underlined and correct words are in parentheses)

1. How many (**much**) furniture is there in your apartment?
2. Can you give me an information (**me information**) about flight (**flights**) to Tokyo?
3. Hurry up! We don't have many times (**much time**) before the show starts.
4. This tabletop is made of a glass (**of glass**), and the legs are made of a wood (**of wood**).
5. I have to write a letter. Can you lend me a paper (**some paper / paper / a piece of paper**) and an envelope?
6. He's going to have his hairs (**hair**) cut and his beards (**beard**) trimmed.
7. I drink tea without a milk (**without milk**) but with slice (**a slice**) of lemon and a sugar (**and sugar / and one sugar / and some sugar**).
8. There's fewer (**less**) traffic downtown today than day (**the day**) before yesterday.

Follow-up

Have students write down two or three sentences, using words from this unit, and pass them to another student to read and check. Collect the papers and read through them to see how the class is doing.

6.5   A few dollars more . . .

Procedure

Before putting everyone in pairs, demonstrate how the conversations might go by using the patterns in the speech balloons. Do the first item with the whole class. For example:

You need more money to pay for a vacation in the Caribbean than in Europe.
- *Not many people can afford to vacation in the Caribbean.*
A vacation in Canada doesn't cost as much as one in Europe.
- *Oh, I don't agree. I think you need a lot more money to go to Canada than Europe.*

Pair work   This is a discussion activity that can be done in groups of 3 if you prefer. During the discussion, go around the class making note of any relevant errors you overhear.

At the end of the discussion, ask some pairs to report back to the whole class. Point out any relevant errors you overheard and call on the class to correct them.

Follow-up

Have the class work in pairs. Ask students to write down five things that cost about $100 and five things that cost about $1 (or an equivalent round number in your students' local currency).

Then students show their list to another pair and ask them to say which things on each list cost more and which cost less.

7 Articles – I

Grammar Summary

Practice in using articles (in some cases no article, or "zero article") to refer to things in general or things in particular:

I love bananas and oranges. (in general)
Fruit is good for you, and oranges are best of all. (in general)
*I'd like **a** banana or **an** orange, please.* (any one)
*Would you like **some** bananas or **some** other fruit?* (any ones)
***The** banana I had was rotten, but **the** orange was good.* (in particular)
I enjoy music and writing letters. (in general)

Using *a* or *an* before names of professions and occupations used in singular form, but not before subjects studied:

*She wants to be **a** doctor. That's why she's studying medicine.*

Relevant errors

✗ She's studying the medicine.
✗ He wants to be doctor.
✗ I like the apples in general.
✗ I need a aspirin.
✗ I love the classical music.
✗ I've finished all work.
✗ The desk is made of the wood.
✗ He works in office.
✗ Their house is by sea.
✗ We enjoy eating some raw fish.

7.1 Do you like fruit?

Warm-up (*3 minutes*)

If possible, bring a small selection of fruit to class, including some apples. With books closed, act out the following dialogue with a student.

Teacher: *Would you like some fruit?*
Student: *Oh, yes, please! I love fruit!*
Teacher: *Well, there are some grapes and some apples.*
Student: *Oh, I'll have some grapes, please.*
Teacher: *Are you sure you won't have an apple, too?*
Student: *No, thanks. Mmm! What delicious grapes!*
Teacher: *Glad you like them. I guess I'll have an apple myself.*

Point out that the word "fruit" is usually uncountable. If you can't bring fruit to class, act out the dialogue anyway, pretending you have the fruit. The dialogue is intended to be humorous, not realistic!

Procedure

A Books are open. Have everyone write the answers in the blanks before going over the exercise as a class. When checking answers with the students, make sure they understand the *reason* for the answers.

ANSWERS
A: *Would you like **an** apple?* (one apple, of the two she is offering)
B: *Oh, yes please! I love Ø* apples.* (apples in general)
A: *Well, there's **a** big one and **a** small one.* (one of each kind)
B: *Oh, I'll have **the** small one please.* (use *the* for a particular apple)
A: *Are you sure you won't have **the** big one?*
B: *No, thanks. Mmm! What **a** delicious apple!*

*Ø = "zero article" (i.e., no article)

A: *Glad you like it. I guess I'll have* **the** *big one myself.*

B *Pair work*   The conversations should be acted out privately, not with the whole class as audience. Have students switch roles at some point so that everyone practices both parts.

C   First, go over the examples with the class, asking for suggestions on how the sentences might continue. For example:

I usually like apples because **they're crisp and juicy**, *but the apple I had yesterday was* **soft and tasteless**.
Usually I hate bananas because **they don't have much flavor**, *but the banana I tried just now was* **absolutely delicious**.
As a rule I love coffee because **it tastes wonderful when it's fresh**, *but the coffee they serve here is* **bitter**.

Then the activity can be done in pairs again or as a whole class.

Follow-up

Have students look around the room they're in – and, if possible, out of the window and door too. Then get each member of the class to think of one thing or group of things she or he has seen. The others have to play "I Spy" and guess what is in the first player's mind. The only clue students have is the first letter of the word. For example:

First player: *This word begins with* T.
Other students: *One of the tables? The top of a pen? The teacher's desk? The Teacher's Manual of* Communicative Grammar Practice? *One of the trees outside?*
First player: *Yes – but which one?*
Other student: *The tree on the right?*
First player: *No.*
Other student: *The one in the middle?*
First player: *That's right. Now it's your turn.*

7.2   Fill in the blanks
Procedure

Go over the example first, and answer any questions about the vocabulary in the exercise. The exercise can be done in pairs in class, or you may want to assign it as homework, as it's the only piece of written work in this unit.

ANSWERS
2. **The** pollution caused by **Ø** cars is worse if **the** cars are driven at **Ø** high speeds.
3. I was watching **a** great movie on **Ø** TV **Ø** last night when **the** TV stopped working.
4. **The** movie I saw was awfully violent – I don't like **Ø** violent movies.
5. **Ø** Good health and **Ø** happiness are more important than **Ø** wealth or **Ø** power. (NOTE: Students should capitalize the first word *good* because there is no article.)
6. **Ø** Washington is **the** capital city of **the** United States, but **Ø** New York is **the** city with **the** largest number of **Ø** inhabitants in **the** country.
7. **Ø** Italian food is great, but **the** pizza I had at **the** restaurant on **the** corner was terrible.
8. She is studying **Ø** history and **Ø** geography – her special interests are **the** history of **Ø** Latin America and **the** geography of **Ø** Canada.

Follow-up

Start a discussion about some of the issues raised in the exercise (in sentences 1, 2, 4, 5, and maybe 7 and 8), and ask students to give their views. For example:

What are the worst forms of pollution in your city?
How do you feel about violence in movies and on TV?
What things are important to you in life?
What kinds of food do you like best?
What subjects are you most interested in?

7.3   Communication activity: How do you feel about . . . ?

Warm-up (*3 minutes*)

Books are closed. Ask students to say how they feel about watching TV. For example:

What kinds of shows do you like best?
What do you do instead of watching TV?
What kinds of shows do you never *watch?*

Procedure

Pair work   Books are open. Student A looks at Activity 4, while Student B looks at 11 (a third student can share Student A's information). This is an open-ended discussion activity. The idea is to talk first about the topics that interest students most, and to leave the less interesting ones until later. The topics can be dealt with in any order.

  Some classes may need to be reminded that this is a give-and-take activity. When Student A asks Student B about a topic, B states a view and then asks A, "What do you think?" before introducing a new topic. Encourage students to say *why* they like or dislike something. For example:

I enjoy watching television. My favorite show is "Wheel of Fortune," a game show. I like to see what the hostess is wearing . . .
I can't stand daytime soap operas. They're all so boring and silly . . .

Follow-up

Ask pairs to tell the rest of the class about the topic they disagreed about most, and to explain how their opinions differed.

7.4   What a job!

Warm-up (*3 minutes*)

Books are closed. Ask the class what professions or occupations they have (or hope to have one day). And ask what other members of their families do.

Procedure

A   *Pair work*   Books are open. To start things off, ask the class to say what a *teacher* does and what a *student* does. Explain that they do lots of different things. Make a list on the board. For example:

What exactly does a teacher do besides "teach" and "grade papers"?
- A teacher assigns homework.
- Teachers have staff meetings.
- A teacher prepares students for examinations.

What exactly does a student do besides "study"?
- Students have to do their homework.
- Students have to do research at the library.
- Some students have to work at a job as well as study.

Then have students do the exercise in pairs. At the end, ask for questions.

B   *Pair work*   Start off by discussing the first two items with the class. Explain to students that they should follow the pattern illustrated in the Student's Book. There are no "correct answers" for this activity. For example:

Would you rather be a doctor or a patient?
- I'd rather be a doctor.
Why?
- Because patients are usually sick. I hate being sick.

Would you rather be a teacher or a student?
- I think I'd rather be a teacher.

Why?
– *Because I don't think they have to do as much work as students.*

At the end, ask pairs to tell the rest of the class about any disagreements they had about the differences.

C *Pair work* Encourage everyone to suggest a variety of jobs or professions the people in the list might have when they get out of school.

SAMPLE ANSWERS
Ann might become a doctor or a nurse.
Tim might become a researcher or a social worker.
Ellen might become a teacher or a professor.
Jack might become a musician or a singer.
Jane might become a lawyer or a judge.
Ed might become a cook or a restaurant manager.
Sue might become a translator, an interpreter, a sales representative or a lecturer.
Bill might become a businessperson or a consultant.

Maria might become a writer or a poet.
Ron might become a computer engineer or a programmer.

Follow-up

1. Put the class in groups and ask them to make a list of the jobs they think are the most: *glamorous, dangerous, dirty, difficult, easy, underpaid, overpaid.*
2. Then get them to report back to the whole class, giving their reasons.

Teachers are the most underpaid.
I think coal miners have the dirtiest job.
Movie actors are the most overpaid workers, I think.
A police officer has the most dangerous job.

If students don't manage to form *dirtiest* and *easiest*, you can give them a little practice with other two-syllable adjectives ending in *y* – for example: *busy, pretty, heavy, noisy, messy, curly.*

8 Articles – II

Grammar summary

Using no article (Ø) with names of continents, most countries,* states, cities, lakes, islands, mountains, and streets:

> Asia   Sweden   California   Chicago
> Lake Ontario   Hokkaido
> Mount McKinley   Broadway
> Hollywood Boulevard   Main Street   etc.

and with many of the important places in a city or state that a tourist might visit (except museums and galleries):

> Fisherman's Wharf   Central Park
> Yosemite National Park   Waikiki Beach
> Alcatraz Island   etc.

*Some exceptions are:

> the USA / United States
> the UK / United Kingdom

Using the with groups of islands, groups of mountains, oceans and seas, rivers, hotels, and museums:

> **the** Canary Islands   **the** Himalayas
> **the** Pacific   **the** Caribbean   **the** Nile
> **the** Sheraton   **the** Smithsonian
> **the** Maritime Museum   etc.

Omitting the or a in some prepositional phrases:

> You should go to bed.
> He's at work.

but not in other prepositional phrases:

> Stop looking out of **the** window.
> I got this at **a** store near me.

Relevant errors

✗ Have you visited the Africa?
✗ The Lake Superior is the largest of the Great Lakes.
✗ They went jogging in the Central Park.
✗ Have you ever seen Pacific Ocean?
✗ Nile is longest river in Africa.
✗ It's time for me to go to the bed.
✗ I spend the most of my time in the meetings.

8.1   Place names

Procedure

Look at part A in the Student's Book and draw the student's attention to the use of *the* or no article (Ø) in the examples.

Ask the class to give one extra example for each group of place names in the list in part A. This will help students who are less knowledgeable about geography to get started later.

Pair work   Have everyone add two or three more examples to each of these lists. Suggest that students include some examples of place names from their own countries.

Check students' spelling – and make sure everyone has used the English forms of the place names.

MORE EXAMPLES	
ISLAND GROUPS	the Bahamas, the Balearic islands, the Seychelles
MOUNTAIN GROUPS	the Appalachians, the Alps, the Sierra Nevada

OCEANS & SEAS	the Sea of Japan, the Caribbean, the Indian Ocean
RIVERS	the St. Lawrence, the Rhine, the Hudson, the Danube
HOTELS	the Hyatt, the Ritz, the Holiday Inn
MUSEUMS & GALLERIES	the Museum of Modern Art, the Prado, the Louvre
COUNTRIES	Canada, Argentina, Greece, Turkey
CONTINENTS	North America, Asia, Australia, Europe
MOUNTAINS	Mount Logan, Mount McKinley, Popocatepetl
ISLANDS	Borneo, Long Island, Jamaica
STREETS	Fifth Avenue, Hollywood Boulevard, Market Street
IMPORTANT PLACES IN A CITY OR REGION	Fisherman's Wharf, City Hall, Central Park
STATES	California, New York, Minnesota (also PROVINCES Ontario, Quebec, British Columbia)
CITIES	Tokyo, Mexico City, Paris, Philadelphia, Minneapolis, Prague
LAKES	Lake Geneva, Lake Superior, Lake Wobegon

B *Group work*   Divide the class into groups of 3 or 4. During this open-ended discussion activity, go around the class listening for and making notes of relevant errors.

Ask each group to come to an agreement on the places they would like or not like to visit. Then, at the end, have each group report to the class on the one place they most want to visit (and why) and the one place they least want to visit (and why).

8.2   The eighties

Warm-up (*1–4 minutes*)

Books are closed. On the board write *1980–89* and ask students: "What do we call this period?" Give the answer if no one knows it, and write *the eighties, the 1980s,* or *the 80s* on the board. Then write *1970–79* and elicit *the seventies.* Do the same for several decades, perhaps as far back as the twenties. Ask students a few questions such as, "What is something that happened in the forties?" (e.g., World War II) or "What are the sixties famous for?" (e.g., hippies, the Beatles).

Procedure

Books are open. Point out that the events listed in the Student's Book are in the form of newspaper headlines. Explain that headlines are a type of title used in newspapers and magazines, and that they differ from complete sentences – articles are usually omitted, and verbs are partially or completely omitted or in the present tense.

Go through the headlines listed and answer any questions about vocabulary. Make sure everyone understands the example, and maybe ask the class to suggest how the first couple of headlines can be rewritten as full sentences.

This exercise can be done together in pairs or by students working alone. Some variations from the sample answers are possible.

SAMPLE ANSWERS
The weather was perfect for the wedding of Charles and Diana in St. Paul's Cathedral in London in 1981.
Compact discs went on sale in record stores for the first time in 1982.
The sales of Michael Jackson's *Thriller* album reached 37 million in 1983.
Archbishop Desmond Tutu of South Africa won the Nobel Peace Prize in 1984.
Mikhail Gorbachev became the leader of the Soviet Union in 1985.

There was an accident at the / a nuclear power station in Chernobyl in 1986.
A painting by van Gogh sold for $53.9 million at an auction in London in 1987.
The total production cost of *Rambo III* was $58 million in 1988. It was the most expensive film ever made.
The Berlin Wall was opened for the first time in 1989.

Follow-up

A   Have students write down some significant events that happened in *their* country during the eighties or nineties. Then ask them to write sentences explaining each one. If you want, students can make their lists together in class and write the sentences as homework.

B   Write the following headlines on the board *one at a time* (each describes a different day and together they tell a story). Have students write a sentence for each headline, explaining what it means.

Japanese expedition to climb Everest this winter
    A Japanese expedition is going to climb Everest this winter.
Members of expedition all women
    The members of the expedition are all women.
Expedition arrives in capital of Nepal
    The expedition has arrived in the capital of Nepal.
Climbers feared lost in storm on mountain
    The climbers are feared lost in a storm on the mountain.
Lost climbers found alive by rescuers
    The lost climbers have been found alive by rescuers.
Climbers return safely to Japan
    The climbers have returned safely to Japan.
Leader of expedition gets own TV show
    The leader of the expedition has gotten her own TV show.

8.3   In bed

Warm-up   (1–2 minutes)

Books are closed. Start by asking the class what they do when they have a cold: "Do you go to bed? Do you go to work / class as usual? see a doctor? take medicine?" and so on.

Procedure

Books are open. Look at the example (sentence 1) together. Explain any unfamiliar vocabulary in the exercise.

Students can work on the exercise alone, but they should compare answers with a partner when they've finished.

ANSWERS
2. Would you like to eat **Ø** lunch at **the** cafe next door, or go to **the** new restaurant downtown?
3. If you want to learn **a** language, is it better to go to **Ø** school or use **a** dictionary?
4. Do you usually eat **a** lot for **Ø** lunch, or do you just have **a** snack?
5. If you look out of **the/a** window in **the** room you're in now, what can you see?
6. What kind of **Ø** music do you like best: **Ø** jazz, **Ø** rock, or **Ø** classical music?
7. Do you know anyone who has been to **the** United Kingdom, **Ø** China, or **the** Soviet Union?
8. Do you come to **Ø** class by **Ø** car, on **Ø** foot, or on **the** bus?

Follow-up

Have students, working in groups of 3 or 4, ask and answer all the questions in the exercise.

As a variation, you can have groups do the exercise as a survey by putting a check mark beside each answer given. At the end, groups count up their checks and report to the class. Together students add the numbers to make "statistics" for the whole class. Then they make sentences, orally and/or in writing, to summarize their findings; for example, "Ten students know someone who has been to the Soviet Union, but only three know someone who has been to the UK," or "Everyone in the class likes rock music best."

8.4 Spot the errors

Procedure

Pair work   To start everyone off, have students look at the first sentence in the exercise and discuss as a class how to correct it. Then divide the class into pairs. While pairs are doing this exercise, circulate around the class offering help as needed.

ANSWERS
1. I love **the / Ø** mountains, and I enjoy **the** seashore too.
2. I have **a** headache and I need **an / some** aspirin.
3. I don't like talking on **the** telephone – I prefer to write **Ø** letters. OR I don't like talking on **the** telephone – I prefer **writing Ø** letters.
4. He's **a** very good friend of mine, even though he has **a** bad temper.
5. She's studying **Ø** music because she wants to become **a** professional musician.
6. I'm going to watch **Ø** TV tonight to see a movie about **Ø / the country** Brazil.
7. I read in **the** newspaper that we're going to have **Ø / some** cold weather.
8. When **the** police arrived, all the people in **the** building were questioned.

Go over the answers with the whole class, making sure students know the reasons for the answers.

Follow-up

Have students look at some recent written work they have done (maybe for Exercise 4.4 or 5.5, part C). Ask them to read through the work quickly to see if they made any errors in the use of *the, a, an,* or *some.* Answer any questions that arise, but don't spend too much time on this.

8.5 A writer's life

Warm-up (*3 minutes*)

Books are closed. Describe a typical day in your own life, along the lines of the paragraph in the Student's Book. Have everyone ask you questions to find out more information.

Procedure

The exercise can be done as homework, or in class with students working in pairs.

ANSWERS
As **a** writer, I seem to spend **Ø** most of **the** time working in my office at **Ø** home, sitting alone in front of **a / the** computer. In fact, **the** only people I see regularly are **the** members of my family when they get home from **Ø** work or **Ø** school. Otherwise, I don't have much contact with **Ø** people, and I'm sorry that I haven't kept in **Ø** touch with **the** friends I made at **Ø** college. I often get **Ø** letters and **Ø** phone calls from **the / Ø** people at **the** publisher's, though, and I try to get out of **the** house at least once **a** day. From **Ø** time to time I give **Ø** lectures or teach **Ø** courses at **Ø** conferences in **Ø** North America or abroad. But if I ever run out of **Ø** ideas or I start suffering from **Ø** loneliness, I'll give up **Ø** writing **Ø** books. Then maybe I'll start **a** new career where I work with lots of **Ø** people and I can have **a** conversation whenever I feel like **Ø** one!

Follow-up

Have students describe a typical day in their own lives. This can be done in class (maybe in groups) and/or in writing as homework. If time permits, students can exchange papers and comment on each other's work.

9 *Comparison*

Grammar summary

Practice in using comparative and superlative forms of adjectives and adverbs:

good	*better*	*the best*
well	*better*	*best*
bad	*worse*	*the worst*
badly	*worse*	*worst*
fast	*faster*	*the fastest*
fast	*faster*	*fastest*
intelligent	*more intelligent*	*the most intelligent*
intelligently	*more intelligently*	*the most intelligently*

Talking about differences, using comparatives and superlatives:

*Brazil is (much) lar**ger than** Greece.*
*Canada is (much) **less** humid **than** Brazil.*
*Greece isn't (quite) **as** cold **as** Canada.*
*Japan is (much) **more** mountainous **than** Uruguay.*

*Jim is **the fattest** boy in the class.*
*Sue is **the most** intelligent person in the class.*
*Tom is **the least** intelligent person I know.*

Using *so, such a, too,* and *enough* in "result clauses":

*The box is **so** heavy **that** I can't lift it.*
*It's **such a** heavy box **that** I can't lift it.*
*It's **too** heavy for me to lift.*
*It's **not** light **enough** for me to lift.*

Relevant errors

✗ Mine is gooder than yours.
✗ Mine is better as yours.
✗ Mine isn't as good than yours.
✗ Mine is more better than yours.
✗ It isn't easy enough that I can do it.
✗ It isn't enough easy that I can do it.

✗ I'm going to work hard more next term.
✗ I'm going to work more hard next term.
✗ This is interestinger than that.
✗ I can run quicklier than you.
✗ It's the best of the world.
✗ It's the less exciting film I've ever seen.
✗ It's the excitingest film I've ever seen.

9.1 Braver than a lion!

Procedure

Looking with the class at the pictures of animals, ask students to identify the various animals shown. To stimulate discussion, some pictures are deliberately ambiguous. The animals are (starting on the left and going down the columns):

tiger	pig
sheep	wasp (or bee?)
bear	horse
camel (or dromedary?)	rabbit
spider	rat (or mouse?)
wolf (or dog?)	parrot (or macaw?)
duck	cow
kangaroo	alligator (or
goat	crocodile?)
bee (or fly?)	fly
mouse (or rat?)	elephant
lion	mosquito
frog (or toad?)	

Making it clear that this is a lighthearted exercise, ask the class to respond to a few questions like these, before getting them to work in pairs:

Do you think a tiger is the same size as a wolf?
Which is bigger: a sheep or a bear?
Which is the largest of them all?
Is a lion bigger than a tiger?

A   *Pair work*   Divide the class into an *even number* of pairs (or groups of 3) for this activity. The idea of the activity is to provoke disagreements and discussion. There are no "correct answers," even though, presumably, everyone would agree that an elephant is the biggest and a mosquito the smallest. During the activity, go around the class listening for relevant errors.

At the end, have each pair join another pair to compare ideas. (There's no need to wait until everyone has come to the very end of their lists!) Point out the errors you overheard before going on to part B.

B   Keep the class divided into an even number of pairs (or groups of 3) for this activity. It's more challenging than part A, so make sure you allow enough time to do it justice. At the end, have each pair join another pair to compare ideas.

Follow-up

Ask the class to suggest some other animals – not shown in the pictures – that are even faster (e.g., cheetah or deer), slower (e.g., turtle or snail), fiercer (e.g., shark), and so on, than the animals shown. Encourage disagreement: "I don't think a deer is faster than a horse." "I think a horse is just as fast as a deer."

Find out which of all the animals in the world students like best and why, and which they like least or fear most.

9.2   More exciting than knitting!

Warm-up   (*1–3 minutes*)

Books are closed. List the following six phrases on the board:

easier than
the easiest
more exciting than
the most exciting

safer than
the safest

Ask students to suggest the opposite of each phrase:

harder than (OR *more difficult than*)
the hardest (OR *the most difficult*)
duller than (OR *less exciting than, more boring than*)
the dullest (OR *the least exciting, the most boring*)
more dangerous than
the most dangerous

Procedure

Books are open. Start off by asking students which of the activities listed is the most difficult and which is the easiest – and why.

Group work   Divide the class into groups of 3 or 4. At the end ask the groups to report on their decisions to the whole class.

Follow-up

"The Comparison Game" is an old favorite that extends the idea of the previous activities and leads in nicely to the next one. The idea is to state the various differences between everyday objects, using comparative sentences. For example, the difference between *a chair* and *a table* might be described in various ways:

A table has longer legs than a chair.
A chair is more comfortable to sit on than a table.
A table is easier to build than a chair.

Here are some ideas to choose from; these can be supplemented with your ideas or ideas from the class:

table – chair	sweater – jacket
gate – door	boots – shoes
fence – wall	car – bus
bank – post office	office – factory
friend – relative	letter – book
movie – video	computer – typewriter
phone – radio	cash – credit cards
pencil – ballpoint pen	

NOTE: To make the game less predictable and more challenging, some of the following words can be "banned" during this activity: *bigger, larger, smaller, better.*

9.3   It's the most . . .

Warm-up

Ask the class to open their books to Exercise 9.3 and give them only 30 seconds to look at the picture of the four people and the sample sentences describing them. Have students close their books; use these questions/instructions:

How many people are there in the picture?
What are their names in order from left to right?
Tell me about Sue/Maria/Jim/Ted. Is Jim the
*   tallest? Is Ted the youngest?* etc.

(If no one in the class can remember a particular answer, let everyone take a quick peek back at the picture, but require that all books be closed again before the answer is given.)

Procedure

Books are closed. Write *apple, grapefruit, pineapple, lemon* on the board. Ask students for statements about each fruit that tell how it's the most (maximum) "something." For example:

An apple is the crunchiest fruit. An apple is the
*   easiest fruit to eat.*
A grapefruit has the most juice. A grapefruit is
*   the hardest one to eat.*
A pineapple is the most prickly fruit. It is the
*   tastiest fruit to eat.*
A lemon is the most sour fruit. A lemon is the
*   easiest fruit to squeeze juice from.*

If necessary, prompt students a little with such questions/instructions as:

Tell me about the outside of the fruit. Think
*   about the taste.*
Are they all easy to eat? Do they all have a lot of
*   juice?* etc.

(Allow time after each prompt for thought and suggestions before giving another prompt.)

Group work   Books are open. Divide the class into groups of 3 or 4. As this is all a matter of opinion, there are no "correct answers." Encourage groups to consult other groups if they can't think of anything to say about some items.

Follow-up

1. Ask the class to name several makes of car and write them on the board. Have them make a statement about each using *the most . . .* or *the -est.*
2. Then ask students to name several cities in their own countries and make statements about each.
3. Finally, ask them to name some famous people and make statements about each, still using *the most . . .* or *the -est.*

9.4   It's much too big!

Procedure

Look at the third cartoon (the elephant cartoon) as a class. Note the four ways of describing it, and ask for more ideas about how to describe the situation. For example:

This van is much too small for this elephant to
*   fit in.*
It's such a small van that we'll have to get a
*   truck if we want to transport the elephant.*

Group work   Divide the class into groups of 3 or 4 for this activity. Make sure everyone in the group – not just one person – writes the sentences.

If the writing load seems too heavy (20 sentences), have groups *talk* about each picture and only write down their most interesting or amusing sentences.

During the activity, go around the class looking at the written sentences. Make on-the-spot corrections of any relevant errors you see or overhear.

SAMPLE ANSWERS

She has such a big foot that the shoe won't fit.
The shoe is too small to go on her foot.
The shoe isn't big enough to fit her foot.
Her foot is so big that the shoe won't fit.

He has such long legs that those pants don't fit him.
He's too tall to wear those pants.
The pants aren't long enough for him to wear.
They're so short that he can't go out in them.

The elephant is far too big to get in the van.
It's such a little van that the elephant won't go in.
The elephant isn't small enough to fit in the van.
An elephant is so big that you can't get it in a small van like that.

The thing in her hand is too small for her to see.
Her eyesight isn't good enough to see what's in her hand.
It's such a tiny object that she can't see it properly.
It's so small that she can't see it very well.

It's such a heavy box that it needs two people to lift it.
The box is too heavy for him to lift.
He's not strong enough to lift the box.
The box is so heavy that he can't lift it.

Follow-up

Divide the class into pairs, each consisting of members of two different groups. Have them compare sentences with each other.

9.5 In other words

Warm-up *(2–3 minutes)*

Books are closed. Write the following sentences on the board to remind students of the patterns they have been practicing earlier in this unit.

My country is .... er than *(name of another country).*
is more .... than
isn't as .... as
is less .... than
is the most .... *in the world / Asia.* etc.

Ask students to describe aspects of their own country by suggesting what adjectives could be used to fill in the blanks.

Encourage everyone not just to fill in the blanks, but to make other comparisons too. For example:

My country is smaller than China.
The scenery in my country is the most beautiful in the world.

Procedure

Books are open. The exercise reviews what students have learned in this unit. It can be assigned as homework or done by students working alone in class. Before you mark the exercise, have students check another student's work. Discuss any variations to the sample answers.

SAMPLE ANSWERS

2. That's the **nicest thing that anyone has ever said to me.**
3. It's **too far for me to walk with my bad leg.**
4. A Boeing 727 **holds fewer passengers than a 747.** OR A Boeing 727 **doesn't hold as many passengers as a 747.**
5. I think coffee **is better than tea.**
6. This shirt isn't **clean enough for me to wear.**
7. Mexico is a **warmer country than Canada.**
8. The population of Korea **is larger / greater than the population of Taiwan.**

Follow-up

If your students all come from the same country, draw a map of that country on the board and ask them to name all the countries surrounding it or nearby. Add these to the map. Ask the class to make statements about all the countries shown (i.e., the geography, the people and the food) using the structures they have learned in this unit.

If students come from different countries, ask them to sketch maps of their respective countries (and neighboring countries) on large paper. The maps and accompanying sentences can be displayed on the wall or bulletin board for the class to look at. Or they can be presented in brief oral reports to small groups or the whole class.

10 Requests and obligation

Grammar summary

Making requests:

Would you mind *opening the door?*
Could you *open the door, please?*
Can you *please open the door?*
I'd like you to *open the door.*
Will you *please open the door?*

Asking for permission:

Would you mind if I *opened the door?*
May I *open the door, please?*
Can I *open the door?*
Do you mind if I *open the door?*
Is it all right if I *open the door?*
Could I *open the door, please?*

Making statements about what is permitted and not permitted (forbidden):

You **can't** *smoke in here.*
You **aren't allowed to** *smoke in here.*
You **aren't supposed to** *smoke in here.*
*You***'d better not** *smoke in here.*
You **can** *smoke outside.*
You **are allowed to** *smoke outside.*
It's all right to *smoke outside.*

Talking (and asking) about obligation and lack of obligation:

You **have to** *fill out this form.*
*You***'ve got to** *fill out this form.*
You **should** *fill out this form.*
You **don't have to** *write in capitals.*
There's no need to *write in capitals.*

Do I have to *use a pen?*
Is there any need to *write in pen?*
Is it necessary to *use a pen?*

Relevant errors

✗ Would you mind to open the door?
✗ Do I must do that?
✗ He musted to do it.
✗ Need I to do that?
✗ You needn't to do that.
✗ I'd like you opening the door.
✗ Please to open the door.
✗ You don't can do that.

Other errors include using an impolite tone of voice, or an unsuitably direct phrase, when talking to someone you don't know well or someone you should address respectfully.

10.1 Would you mind . . . ?

Warm-up (5–10 minutes)

1. Start by borrowing a variety of objects from the class (pens, pencils, books, watches, etc.), using the expressions given in the Student's Book. Place the borrowed objects in a row on the table in front of you. For example:

Tony, do you mind if I take your dictionary for a couple of minutes?
Kumiko, would you mind if I borrowed your eraser for a moment?

2. Now tell the class to ask you to give each one back. Encourage them to use the expressions given in the activity. For example:

Could you give me my pen back, please?
Would you mind giving my watch back, please?

3. Now have the students ask other students for permission to borrow or look at their property, again using the expressions given. For example:

Hiroshi, do you mind if I look at your watch?
Carmen, is it all right if I borrow your pen for a moment?

4. Remind students that politeness is expressed by the tone of voice you use, not just by the words. For example, if "Could you lend me your pen?" is spoken rapidly with little variation in pitch, it sounds rude. If it's spoken more slowly with a rising intonation, it sounds polite. Demonstrate this to the class.

5. Point out to students that the *positive* responses to *"Would you mind (if I) . . ."* and *"Do you mind if I . . . ?"* questions are *negative* in form, that is, *"Not at all,"* and *"No, of course not."*

Also, point out that the *-ing* form is required after *"Would you mind . . . ?"* and the past verb form ("past" in form but not in meaning) follows *"Would you mind if I . . . ?"*

Procedure

Divide the class into groups of 3. For the purposes of this exercise, have students assume that they are talking to an acquaintance (someone they don't know very well) and decide together what they would say. (All the expressions given in the Student's Book are suitable for this situation.)

They should write down one sentence they think is most suitable for each situation. Go around the class making on-the-spot corrections of any relevant errors in the written sentences. There are no "correct answers," but discuss any problems that arise with the class.

Follow-up

Have the class act out what they'd say in each situation, with you (or one of the students) playing the part of the "acquaintance." For example:

Would you mind if I turned on a light? I'd like to read the paper, and the room is too dark.
– No, of course not. Go right ahead.

Is it all right if I borrow your dictionary? I'm having trouble with my homework assignment.
– Certainly. But could you please return it by tomorrow? I'll need it for class.

10.2 Communication activity: I'd like you to . . .

Warm-up *(1–2 minutes)*

Begin by getting the class to do some physical exercises, using the phrases shown in the Student's Book. For example:

First of all, I'd like you all to stand up.
Now, will you please put your hands by your sides?
I want you to stand up very straight with your head up high.
Now can you raise your right arm up in front of you?
Would you mind doing the same with your left arm?
Now I'd like you to very slowly bend your knees, keeping your arms out in front of you.
Can you stay like that until I count to five?
Now could you slowly straighten your knees and return to a standing position?

Procedure

Pair work   Student A looks at Activity 13, while Student B looks at 21. They'll be following each other's instructions, which may involve standing up, raising arms, and closing eyes. Nothing energetic is called for, but if there is unused space anywhere in the room, it would be a good idea to move some of the students into it.

As you walk around the room listening to the pairs, make sure students are using *requests* like the ones in Exercise 10.1, and not just simple commands. Make sure they use a variety of expressions.

53

Follow-up

Have students tell you what to do, using ideas similar to the pair work activity. If you can't do, or don't feel like doing, any of the things suggested, you could say "I'm afraid I can't do that" or "Sorry, I'd rather not do that."

10.3   Make yourself at home!

Warm-up   *(1–3 minutes)*

Books are closed. Write *strict* on the board and ask students, "What does a strict teacher do?" (gives hard tests, doesn't allow talking, never accepts late papers, etc.). Next write *easygoing* on the board and ask, "What does an easygoing teacher do?" (lets students talk more, accepts answers on tests that aren't exact, etc.). Then ask: "Which is better – an easygoing teacher or a strict one? Why or why not?" Finally, as a transition to the book exercise, tell students: "We've been talking about easygoing and strict teachers. Now we're going to talk about easygoing and strict roommates."

Procedure

Books are open. Explain the situation to the class, asking for suggestions on some of the "rules" that a very strict roommate might have. It may help to think of the different rooms in the imaginary apartment, and the rules that would apply in each one.

Divide the class into pairs or groups of 3. After discussing the situation, they should write their eight sentences. As you go around the class, make on-the-spot corrections of any relevant errors in the sentences.

SAMPLE ANSWERS
You can listen to the radio if you keep the volume low.

You can't watch TV after 10 p.m.
It's all right to use the washing machine, but not early in the morning.
You'd better not use the kitchen in the evening.
You're allowed to take a shower in the morning.
You can't take a bath in the evening.
If you want you can put things in the refrigerator, but only on the top shelf.
You aren't supposed to use the phone.
You aren't allowed to smoke anywhere in the apartment.

Follow-up

Have students work in groups. Ask them to imagine that a friend is coming to stay for two weeks. What "rules" would they give to a *real* friend? After a few minutes, have groups report back to the class.

10.4   Enjoy your flight!

Procedure

Find out which members of the class have flown before. It may help to arrange groups so that each one contains at least one experienced air traveler – though this is not essential. Go over any unfamiliar vocabulary.

A   *Group work*   Divide the class into groups of 3 or 4. They should begin by placing a check mark next to the permitted items. Then they can talk about what is permitted or not. For example:

You can't take a pet onto an airplane, not even a small one.
You're certainly allowed to take a briefcase on board.
Yes, but if you already have a large handbag, are you allowed to have a briefcase too?

If students need cues, write these on the board: *You can/can't . . . , You're certainly allowed to . . . , You're not allowed to . . .*

SAMPLE ANSWERS

The only things that are *not* allowed are a pair of skis, a pet, a briefcase and a guitar (although in theory, these last two items both count as an extra carry-on bag), and a stroller. A large lap-top computer might also count as an extra carry-on bag.

You probably wouldn't be allowed to take a large pile of books or one each of all the "permitted" items!

B *Group work*   Students should remain in the same groups for this activity. No specialist knowledge of air travel is required to do this, provided that students use their common sense and think of the airplane scenes they've seen in movies. For example:

As far as I know, you can drink on an airplane.
– Yes, but you can't drink when it's taking off.
– And you aren't allowed to drink when it's landing.
– And I don't think you're allowed to drink after it's landed.

The activities that are not permitted are:

drinking during takeoff and during or after landing (although it's allowed during the flight)
smoking (when the "No Smoking" sign is on, in a no smoking area, in the aisle, in the lavatory) – some airlines don't allow smoking at all on any of their flights
opening doors and windows
playing ball
standing up when the "Fasten Seat Belt" sign is on
undoing your seat belt when the "Fasten Seat Belt" sign is on
running
walking around when the "Fasten Seat Belt" sign is on
singing (but only if it annoys fellow passengers)

Follow-up

Discuss with the class which of the activities in part B are permitted/forbidden on a train, bus, subway, ship; in a taxi, classroom, church; and so on.

10.5   Do I have to . . . ?

Warm-up *(2–3 minutes)*

If your students are learning English in their own country, tell them how strange it feels for a foreigner who has just arrived to get used to living in an unfamiliar new country. It isn't just the language, but also the climate, the habits of the people, the traffic, and the public transportation system that can make you feel you've set foot on a different planet. Things that a native takes for granted are often puzzling, or even frightening, for a newly arrived visitor. (If you're a foreigner in their country, tell them about your own experiences.)

If your students are studying in an English-speaking country, or if they have lived in other countries, find out about their first experiences of life in a new country.

Procedure

Divide the class into groups of 3 or 4. To start them off, choose one of the topics listed in the Student's Book and ask the class what questions a visitor might have and what advice they'd give. Encourage them, of course, to use the phrases shown in the Student's Book. For example, if you're discussing social behavior:

Is it necessary to remove my shoes before I enter someone's home?
– Yes, you should take them off and leave them at the front door.
Do I need to arrive on time for an appointment?
– Yes, it's a good idea to arrive on time or a few minutes early.
Should I bring a gift for my hosts?
– Yes, it's a good idea to bring something from your own country.

Allow plenty of time for this activity – it can be very productive and enlightening. And allow time at the end for an exchange of ideas as a class.

Follow-up

1. Divide the class into pairs, consisting of members of different groups from the ones in Exercise 10.5. One person plays the role of "foreign visitor" and asks questions about customs and habits in the other's country. The other has to advise the "visitor." (In a multinational class, pair up students from different countries – then neither has to play a role.)

2. After a few minutes, have the members of the pair change roles. For homework, have students write a letter to their friend giving their advice.

3. If your students know enough about life in the United States, Canada, Australia, or Britain, have them discuss what advice they'd give a person from their country who is going to one of these countries for the first time. They could role-play this in the same way as in (1).

10.6   In other words . . .

Procedure

If you think your students will have difficulty with the exercise, discuss how the first example might be done. Remind them that they can use phrases from the entire unit. This exercise can be assigned as homework or done by students together in pairs.

SAMPLE ANSWERS

1. You aren't **allowed / supposed to chew gum in class.**

2. Do I **have to attend every class?**
3. Is **it all right to bring my dog to class?**
4. **I'd like you to open your books to page 13.**
5. There**'s no need to wear a suit for school.**
6. Would **you mind if I left early today?**
7. Would **you mind passing out these books please?**
8. You don't **have to take exams.**

Follow-up

1. Prepare slips of paper with the names of different occupations; for example, *painter, president, singer, police officer, gardener.*

2. Each member of the class chooses one slip; and doesn't show it to anyone. Students have to pretend that this is their real job.

3. Each student is questioned by the others, who try to find out about the occupation by asking only questions beginning:

Can you . . . ? (e.g., Can you work outside?)

Do you have to . . . ? (e.g., Do you have to work with your hands?)

Are you allowed to . . . ? (e.g., Are you allowed to dress in jeans?)

Are you supposed to . . . ? (e.g., Are you supposed to wear a uniform?)

Are you expected to . . . ? (e.g., Are you expected to work on weekends?)

Only "yes" and "no" answers are allowed.

4. After two or three rounds, you can speed things up by dividing the class into groups and having them continue the game in the same way. Additional slips can be given to groups who finish quickly.

11 Ability

Grammar summary

Making statements about ability and inability:

Can you *swim?*
Do you know how to *use a word processor?*
Were you able to *finish your work?*

You **can** *swim, but I* **can't.**
I'm **unable to** *swim.*
I'll **be able to** *swim by the end of the summer.*
I wish I could *swim as well as you can.*
It'd be nice to be able to *swim.*

I **was able to** *jump across the stream.*
I **wasn't able to** *step over it.*
I **managed to** *jump across the stream.*
I **didn't manage to** *step over it.*
I **couldn't** *step over it.*

Describing how one would get help to do things:

I'd need someone to help me *prepare a four-course meal for 12 guests.*
I'd get someone to *do the dishes afterwards.*
I'd have *the menus printed for me.*

Relevant errors

✗ I don't can do that.
✗ He managed doing it.
✗ I have done that by a mechanic.
✗ Could you get the carrots yesterday?
✗ She can't to swim very well.

11.1   Evening classes

Warm-up *(1–2 minutes)*

Books are closed. If appropriate, ask the class:

Has anyone ever taken evening classes? (What did you take? Tell us about it.)

Where can you take evening classes?
What subjects can you take in evening classes?

Tell the class any of your own experiences in taking or teaching evening classes.

Procedure

Books are open. Look at the cartoons with the class and answer any questions about vocabulary. Pick one of the evening classes from the list and ask the class to suggest how the sentences in the speech balloons would continue. For example, talking about the French class:

I can't speak French. I wish I could speak French. It'd be nice to be able to speak French.
By the end of the course, I'll be able to take part in a conversation in French. If I work hard, I'll learn enough French to be able to take part in a conversation.
Now I can speak French fairly well, but six months ago I couldn't speak a word.

Every student should imagine enrolling in the evening courses listed. Ask the class to make up more sentences about the courses, discussing their abilities before and after. When everyone seems to have the idea, compare sentences as a class and correct any relevant errors.

Pair work   First, elicit from the class ideas for other evening courses, such as business correspondence, singing, or photography. Then divide the class into pairs or groups of 3. After students add extra evening classes to the list, they should use the same patterns to talk about them.

At the end, bring the class back together for a minute or two. Quickly ask the various groups to tell which courses they would really like to take, whether from the list in the Student's Book or their own lists. See if any groups had the same ideas.

Follow-up

1. Divide the class into an *even* number of groups of 3 or 4 (or pairs).
2. Ask members of each group to devise a questionnaire to find out about the abilities of another group's members. Give some examples of the kind of questions they can ask to get the required information:

COOKING: *Can you bake a cake? make a soufflé? fry an omelette?*

DRIVING: *Can you drive a car? a van? a bus?*

RIDING: *Can you ride a horse? a bike? a motorcycle? a camel?*

CLIMBING: *Can you climb over a wall? up a tree? up a mountain?*

RUNNING: *Can you run 100 meters? 1000 meters? 100 kilometers?*

etc.

3. When all the groups have composed a set of questions, combine everyone into double-size groups ("Group A" and "Group B").
4. Each person in Group A is asked the questions in Group B's questionnaire, and vice versa. One member of each group keeps a record of the answers by marking a check (✓) on the questionnaire for each "yes" answer and a cross (✗) for each "no" answer.
5. Reports are given to the rest of the class, like this:

All of them can ride a bike, one of them can ride a horse, and three of them can ride a motorbike. Three of them can't ride a camel, but one of them can.

11.2 Communication activity: Shopping lists

Warm-up (*1–2 minutes*)

Books are closed. Ask students:

Who does the grocery shopping for you?

Do you/they make a list?
Do you/they actually remember what to get?
Do you/they buy things that aren't on the list?

Procedure

Books are open. Answer any questions about the vocabulary in the shopping lists. Write these phrases on the board:

Did you manage to get . . . ?
I didn't manage to get . . .
I managed to get . . .
Were you able to get . . . ?
I wasn't able to get . . .
I couldn't get . . .
I was able to get . . .

Students should use these phrases when they are doing the activity later.

Point out that *Could you get any eggs?* and *I could get some eggs* are not correct in this context. (*Could you get some eggs?* is a request – see Unit 10; *I could get some eggs* indicates possibility– see Unit 18.)

Pair work   Student A looks at Activity 23, while Student B looks at 28. Make sure everyone understands the instructions. During this activity, go around the class and make on-the-spot corrections of any relevant errors.

Follow-up

Find out about shopping that students have really done recently. Ask what they intended to buy, or what was on their shopping lists. Have them tell the class what they were able/weren't able to buy.

11.3 Success at last!

Warm-up (*2–3 minutes*)

Books are closed. As the class watches, act out or mime an action (touching the ceiling, opening a stuck window, throwing paper across the room into the wastebasket, etc.), but *fail*.

Write *could, manage, able to* on the board and elicit a sentence about your unsuccessful action using each:

You couldn't touch the ceiling.
You didn't manage to touch the ceiling.
You weren't able to touch the ceiling.

Then act out something and *succeed*. Elicit sentences with *manage* and *able to*:

You were able to open the window.
You managed to open the window.

Procedure

Books are open. Before everyone starts writing, ask the class to suggest some more sentences they could write about the first picture. For example:

He couldn't open the door.
He managed to get in the apartment through an open window.
He was able to open the door easily the next day.

A   Students can work together in pairs, or this activity can be done by students working alone. Go around the class correcting any relevant errors you see.

Ask everyone to compare sentences with another student, or pair, at the end. Answer any questions that arise.

SAMPLE ANSWERS
She was able to lift the heaviest weight. / She managed to beat all the other competitors.
They managed to put up the tent. / They were able to follow the instructions that came with the tent.
He managed to get to the top of the mountain. / He was able to reach the peak without difficulty.
He didn't manage to catch the bus. / He wasn't able to get to the bus stop before the bus left.
She couldn't reach the book. / She didn't manage to get the book from the top shelf.

B   Again, this can be done by students working together in pairs or alone. Ask everyone to compare sentences with another student, or pair, at the end.

Follow-up

1. Ask students to tell the rest of the class about their partner's recent successes.
2. Remind a more advanced class that *succeed* is often followed by *in*, as in these examples:

*She **succeeded in** winn**ing** the race.*
*He **didn't succeed in** finish**ing** his work.*

11.4   Do-it-yourself
Procedure

Begin by telling the class about some of the things in the list that you can/can't do. For example:

I can't paint a ceiling because it hurts my back. So I'd get a painter to do that for me. But I can iron a shirt, although I don't like doing it.

Elicit or model as many sentences as possible using the expressions listed. Then deal with any questions about vocabulary in the boxed phrases.

A   *Pair work*   Divide the class into pairs or groups of 3. Have students put a check mark beside the things in the list that their partner can do, so that they can remember their partner's abilities when they do part B. Go around the class making note of any relevant errors you overhear. Discuss the errors you overheard with the class.

B   Students write five sentences about things their partner can do. When they are done, read the items from the box to the class. After you've read an item, ask for a volunteer to make a sentence using one of the listed expressions. Students may want to refer to the sentences they wrote about their partner's skills. For example:

Teacher: *Paint a ceiling.*
Student 1:   *I can do that myself. I love to paint and work around the house.*
Teacher: *Tune a piano.*

Student 2: *I have no idea how to tune a piano!*
           I'd get someone to do that for me.
Teacher: *Build new shelves.*
Student 3: *I don't know how to build shelves,*
           but Rita does. I'd ask her to help me.
etc.

Follow-up

Find out what other practical skills, not shown in the list, each member of the class possesses.

Then get others to give their reactions. For example:

Student 1: *I can translate a letter from Korean*
           into Japanese.
Student 2: *I wish I could do that – I'd have to*
           hire a translator to do that for me.
           Or maybe I could get you to do it for
           me.

12 *Advice and suggestions*

Grammar summary

Asking for advice:

*Should I **invite** him to the party?*
*Is it worth **inviting** him?*
*I can't decide whether **to invite** him.*
*Do you think I should **invite** him?*
*Would it be a good idea **to invite** him?*
*I'm wondering whether **to invite** him.*
*Do you think I ought **to invite** him?*

Giving advice and making suggestions:

*If I were you I'**d see** the doctor.*
*I think you ought **to see** the doctor.*
*My advice is **to see** the doctor.*
*You'd better **see** the doctor.*
*I'd advise you **to see** the doctor.*
*You could **see** the doctor.*
*Why don't you **see** the doctor?*
*You should **see** the doctor.*

Advising someone *not* to do something:

*If I were you I **wouldn't invite** her.*
*I don't think you ought **to invite** her.*
*It'd be better **not to invite** her.*
*You shouldn't **invite** her.*
*It isn't a good idea **to invite** her.*
*I'd advise you **not to invite** her.*

Relevant errors

✗ What I should do?
✗ Is it worth to do that?
✗ If I were you I'll do that.
✗ Why you don't do that?
✗ You'd better to do that.
✗ Should I to do that?
✗ Do you think should I do that?
✗ I can't decide if to do that or not.
✗ My advice is doing that.
✗ You don't better do that.
✗ I think you don't ought to do that.

12.1   What should I do?

Procedure

Begin by asking the class what the person in the cartoon might be thinking, using the structures shown in the Student's Book – it's raining and he has to get to work. For example:

Should I take the bus or a taxi?
Is it worth paying for a taxi to avoid getting wet?
I can't decide whether to call a taxi or to stand in the rain waiting for the bus.
I'm wondering whether to take a taxi or not.
Would it be a good idea to take a taxi since it's raining so hard?
Do you think I ought to take the bus or call a taxi?

A   *Pair work*   This exercise introduces some of the grammatical problems associated with asking for advice, in particular using *-ing* and *to . . .* – see also Units 13 and 14.

Divide the class into pairs or groups of 3. Encourage students to write examples using the full range of expressions, and not stick to the "easiest" ones. There are numerous "correct answers" possible because there are so many ways of asking for advice in the situations shown. While the pairs are working, go around making any on-the-spot corrections necessary.

B   Have students work alone for a minute or two as they write down some more topics they'd like advice on. Then they should rejoin their partner or group and ask for advice, again using the expressions. Write "I think you ought to . . ." on the board and have students use it to respond to their partner's questions. For example:

I can't decide whether to read a book tonight or rent a video.

– *I think you ought to read a book. You watch too many videos!*

If your students can't think of any more topics, you could suggest some of these:

Read a book tonight or rent a video?
Have a snack at lunchtime or a full meal?
Look for a new job or keep this one?
Write a letter to my friend or phone?

Or you could brainstorm more ideas as a whole class. Then have pairs ask each other for advice using the structures they have learned.

Follow-up

With a more advanced class, consider the changes in word order necessary when a request for advice is preceded by *Do you think . . . ?*:

Do you think it's worth writing this down?
Do you think it would be a good idea to make notes?
What do you think I should do?

12.2   If I were you . . .

Warm-up *(1–3 minutes)*

Books are closed. Write *job application* and *job interview* on the board and ask the class:

What is a job application?
What is a job interview?

Perhaps someone can tell you (or you can tell the class) something like this:

It's a form you fill out when you want a job. It gives information about you and your work experience.
It's a conversation you have with an employer when you want a job.

Tell students about a job application you once filled out and/or a job interview you had. Then ask:

What should you wear to a job interview? Are your clothes important?   (Yes, your clothes

are important! You want to make a good impression. It's worth the effort to dress appropriately.)

Procedure

Books are open. Ask the class to look at the illustration: Several people are standing in line for job applications. Joe, who is badly dressed, is one of them. The others are giving Joe advice. Students should imagine that Joe is a friend of theirs. Ask what advice they'd give him. Encourage them to use the structures shown in the Student's Book. Correct any relevant errors that are made.

Then divide the class into pairs and have them continue discussing what advice to give Joe. For practice, students can start with the advice that's already been given in the warm-up. They should write down eight sentences, each using a different structure. For example:

If I were you I'd get a haircut.
You should shave.
I think you ought to wear better clothes.
You'd better get a suit.
Why don't you comb your hair and shave?
You could improve your image.
I'd advise you to go home and change.
My advice is to forget about this interview and look your best for the next one.

Follow-up

Tell the class about some more of Joe's habits.

He also . . .
– always arrives late for interviews
– sleeps late
– only eats hamburgers and potato chips
– has dirty shoes
– spends every evening watching TV
– is in terrible shape
– smokes cigarettes
– is lazy

Ask students to say the advice they'd give Joe.

12.3   If you ask me . . .

Warm-up *(2–3 minutes)*

Books are closed. Write the first three expressions from the list in part A on the board. Tell students to imagine that their friend is having trouble at work and wants to look for a new job. Ask students what they might say to their friend, using the expressions on the board. For example:

I don't think you ought to leave just yet. Maybe you should wait and try to solve your problems at work first.
It isn't a good idea to look for a job when you're upset. It's hard to make good decisions.
If I were you I wouldn't make any decision without really thinking about what I wanted to do for a career.

Procedure

A   Books are open. Explain the situation to the class. Ask students to write down some things they would say to their friend. For example:

I don't think you ought to leave your job.
You shouldn't take this too seriously – things will get better soon.
It isn't a good idea to leave your job before you have another one.
If I were you I wouldn't tell my boss how I felt.
I don't advise you to leave your job if you don't actually have another one.

B   Have the class work in groups of 3, or in pairs, for this part. Encourage them to say *why* they give their advice. For example:

I don't think you should swim from France to England, because the English Channel is too rough.
It isn't a good idea to write your autobiography

because you're still too young. You ought to wait until you're older.

At the end, ask groups to report to the rest of the class on what they'd say.

If there's time, each group or pair could take turns role-playing the two or three friends, asking for and giving advice. If the class needs guidance, write on the board:

A: *I'm thinking of . . .*
B: *Well,* (not a good idea.) (Explain why.)
A: *Hmm. What are* you *thinking of doing these days?*
etc.

Follow-up

1.   Ask the class to say at least ten countries that students have visited, or that they know something about. Write them up on the board. In a multinational class, include all the countries represented in the class.
2.   Divide the class into an even number of pairs or groups of 3.
3.   Ask the pairs or groups to choose six countries they'd advise friends to visit if they have the chance. Ask them to decide on *two* places in each country that are well worth visiting and *one* place that's not worth going to on a short visit.
4.   Combine the pairs into groups of 4 or 6.
5.   Students give their advice about which places to visit and which not to bother visiting. For example:

If I were you I'd go to Brazil, if you have the chance. You ought to go to Rio I think, and it'd be a good idea to go to Salvador, but I don't think you should go to Brasília if you don't have much time.

6.   Reassemble the class and ask them what advice they'd give to someone who is planning a one-week visit to the country or region they're studying in. Play the role of "foreign visitor" yourself, or have one member of the class play this role.

12.4   That's easier said than done

Warm-up (*2–3 minutes*)

Books are closed. Start by telling the class that you feel terribly bored when you're not working. Ask them to suggest what you should do. Reply by explaining the drawbacks of their suggestions, using these phrases:

That's easier said than done, because . . .
That's a good idea, but . . .

For example:

I get so bored when I'm not working.
– Why don't you go to a movie?
That's easier said than done, because I don't
* have enough money to afford it.*
– Why don't you join us for a game of tennis?
That's a good idea, but I don't know how to play.

Procedure

Group work   Books are open. Divide the class into groups of 3 or 4. Each student has to play the role of one of the people shown in the Student's Book. They must ask their partners for advice and turn down advice they don't like, using the expressions given. Before starting, students should spend a few moments thinking about their roles so that they are in the right mood for it.

Tell students how long they have for this activity and that you'll give a signal when they should change roles. Listen to the various groups and, at the end, tell the class the relevant errors that you heard.

Follow-up

Here are some more problems the groups can help each other to solve:

I need to be more physically fit.
I don't know what to do at the end of this
* course.*

I can't decide what kind of career to have.
I want to learn another subject or skill, but I
* don't know which one.*

12.5   People with problems

Procedure

A *Pair work*   Allow a few moments for everyone to read the letters in the Student's Book (they are just extracts, not complete letters).

Divide the class into pairs or groups of 3. Ask them to discuss the topic of each letter and identify the problem exactly. For example, the letter by Chris is about his heavy smoking and his inability to stop. The letter by Lee is about whether to accept a promotion that would mean leaving friends and moving to a new place – New York. After students have identified the topics, have them decide what advice they'd give to each friend.

Have some of the pairs report their ideas to the whole class, and ask for comments.

B   Ask half the class to write a reply to one letter and ask the other half to reply to the other. This can be done as homework.

When students have written their letters, divide the class into pairs, consisting of students who have written letters to the *same* person. Have them compare letters, discussing the advice they gave and checking each other's work. If time allows, collect the letters and read several aloud to the class. With the class, decide if all the advice is basically the same or if some is unique.

Follow-up

A   This activity is a follow-up to part B.
1. "Deliver" each letter from part B to a student who wrote a *different* one. Have them read the letter and reply to it in the role of "friend with a problem," thanking their friend for the advice and maybe pointing out drawbacks.

2. Deliver the replies to the people who wrote the advice in the first place.

VARIATION: After reading the letters, students could work in pairs and role-play a phone call between the two friends.

B   For this activity, collect some real letters written to a magazine or newspaper advice column. Divide the class into groups of 3 or 4. Pass one letter to each group and have them write a reply to it.

Then each letter and reply is passed to another group who comment on the advice given.

13 | *Doing* or *to do?* – *I*

Grammar summary

Practice in using *-ing* forms as the subject of a sentence, or as part of a phrase that acts as the subject:

Swimming *is my favorite sport.*
Being criticized *is unpleasant.*

Using *to* . . . (the infinitive) after adjectives:

It's fun **to swim** *in the ocean.*
It's unpleasant **to be** *criticized.*

Using *-ing* forms after a preposition:

She climbed up **without** *hold***ing** *on.*
He opened it **by** *hold***ing** *it firmly.*

Using verbs that are usually followed by *-ing:*

> avoid   enjoy   detest   finish   keep
> etc.

I **enjoy** *listen***ing** *to music and read***ing** *books.*

Using verbs that are usually followed by *to* . . . :

> choose   learn   manage   mean
> need   etc.

I've **learned to** *type and* **to** *use a computer.*

Using verbs that are usually followed by an object + *to* . . . .

> allow   encourage   force   help
> invite   teach   etc.

He **encouraged me to** *do it.*
They **forced her to** *answer the questions.*

Using verbs that can be followed either by *-ing* or *to* . . . with no different meaning:

> begin   start   like   continue   etc.

It **began to** *rain.*
It **began** *rain***ing.**

Relevant errors

✗ He avoided to do it.
✗ She managed doing it.
✗ I can't sneeze without to close my eyes.
✗ I enjoy to watch sports on TV.
✗ They encouraged me doing it.

13.1   It's easy to . . .

Warm-up *(1–3 minutes)*

Books are closed. Ask the class to say what (apart from going to the movies) they think is "fun" or "great," using *-ing* or *to* . . . in their answers. For example:

Eating ice cream is great!
It's fun to eat ice cream!
Swimming in the ocean is fun!
It's great to be appreciated!

If the class needs visual cues, write *It's fun / great to* . . . and . . . *-ing* . . . *is fun / great* on the board.

Procedure

A   Books are open. Have everyone complete the sentences, working together in pairs. For each item, students should write one sentence with *-ing* (on the left side) and one with *to* . . . (on the right side). Ask the pairs to show another pair what they've written before you go through the exercise with the class.

SAMPLE ANSWERS
2. **Writing a 150-word composition** is easy.
   It isn't hard **to write a 150-word composition.**

3. **Going to the beach on weekends** is enjoyable.
   It's nice **to go to the beach on weekends.**
4. **Meeting strangers** is embarrassing.
   It's embarrassing for me **to meet strangers.**
5. **Being criticized** is awful.
   It's terrible **to be criticized.**

B   This can be done individually or in pairs. Give an example to start everyone off: *It's terrible to miss an English class.* Have everyone compare their sentences with another student or another pair at the end.

Follow-up

Write these expressions on the board:

It's easier to .... *than to* ....
It's harder to .... *than to* ....
I think that .... ing *is easier than* .... ing.
I believe that .... ing *is harder than*
    .... ing.

Ask the class to suggest how each blank might be filled. Then have students, working individually or in pairs, compose their own sentences using the expressions.

13.2   Without blinking

Warm-up *(3–5 minutes)*

Begin by telling the class some of the things you are *interested in* and *afraid of*. For example:

I'm interested in collecting stamps.
*I'm afraid of being attacked by giant plants from
    outer space.*

Then ask students what kinds of things they are *interested in* and *afraid of* – funny sentences rather than real fears might be better. If they say something like "I'm interested in art museums," point out that if they want to include a verb, they need to use *-ing*. For example:

I'm interested in going to art museums.
I'm interested in seeing art museums.

Explain that after a preposition (e.g., *in* or *of*) *-ing*, not *to . . .* , is used – for example, *interested in dancing, tired of working.*

Procedure

A   Before starting the exercise, ask the class to tell you some common prepositions (*in, of, for, to,* etc.). Then have everyone quickly circle the preposition that precedes each blank in the exercise (*without, after, in, of, about, in, for*). The exercise can be done by students working together in pairs, or by students working alone and later comparing answers in pairs.

SAMPLE ANSWERS
2. I had an upset stomach after **eating** oysters.
3. Are you interested in **coming / going** to the beach with us?
4. I'd like to go to Europe, but I'm afraid of **flying / traveling**.
5. We were very disappointed about **losing** the game.
6. I drove very fast, but I didn't succeed in **catching** the plane.
7. Thank you very much for **giving** me such a nice gift.

B   *Pair work*   First, ask students if they can keep their eyes open without blinking – get them to try! Then divide the class into an even number of pairs (or groups of 3). When they have completed the sentences, make sure there's time for them to join another pair (or group) and ask the questions.

The following answers are samples only – your students are likely to come up with some more amusing examples!

SAMPLE ANSWERS
2. Can you touch your toes without **bending your knees?**
3. Can you stop hiccups by **holding your breath / drinking cold water?**
4. Can you cure a cold by **drinking lemon juice / staying in bed?**
5. Can you write a letter in English without **making any mistakes / using a dictionary?**

6. Do you always brush your teeth after **eating / having a meal / eating breakfast?**
7. Do you ever make notes before **writing a letter / writing an essay?**

Follow-up

Form groups of 3 or 4 students and ask them to write more questions like those in part B – the more amusing the challenge, the better. For example:

Can you stand on one leg for 60 seconds without losing your balance?
Can you draw a picture of an animal without lifting your pen off the paper?
Can you balance a pen upright on your hand without dropping it?

After about five minutes, ask groups to report to the rest of the class on the most amusing challenges.

13.3   Verbs + -*ing* or *to . . .*

Warm-up *(2–3 minutes)*

Books are closed. On the board write *I enjoy . . . -ing . . .* and *I dislike . . . -ing . . .* Ask the class to say some of the things they *enjoy doing* and *don't enjoy doing*. For example:

I enjoy going to the movies.
I dislike driving in the city.

Procedure

A   Books are open. Allow a few moments for everyone to study the lists. Make sure everyone understands all the verbs listed.

NOTE: The verbs listed in part A are *usually* followed by -*ing* or *to . . .* as indicated, but some of them can be used with a different form, with a slight change in meaning. For example, although we say, "They won't allow him to swim in the river" and "He isn't allowed to swim in the river," we can also say "They don't

allow swimming in the river" and "Swimming in the river isn't allowed."

With a more advanced class, perhaps explain the difference between "I can't help doing that" and "I can't help you do that / I can't help you to do that":

*I can't help clos**ing** my eyes when I sneeze.*   (I can't avoid closing them. It's impossible to keep them open.)
*I can't help you **do** (or **to do**) your homework – you'll have to do it alone.*

B   This exercise can be done by students working together in pairs, or alone.

ANSWERS
2. **He was pretending to be a police officer.**
3. **We can't afford to buy that new video.**
4. **I dislike watching TV every night.**
5. **I'm going to put off writing those letters (until tomorrow).**
6. **I can't help thinking about my problems all the time.**
7. **I want to invite them to visit our home.**
8. **I didn't mean to step on your foot.**
9. **I miss being with my family.**
10. **They keep interrupting the class.**

C   *Pair work*   Divide the class into an even number of pairs. (This exercise should be done by students working together in pairs.)

Encourage students to complete the sentences with interesting or amusing ideas – just writing *to do it* or *doing it* in every case won't help them to remember the grammar points, and would be pretty boring for another pair to read. While they're doing this, go around the class offering advice and making on-the-spot corrections as necessary.

At the end, form groups of four (pairs of pairs) and have everyone compare sentences.

SAMPLE ANSWERS
2. After finishing their meal, they decided **to have coffee before washing the dishes.**
3. Because of the fog at the airport, we expect **to be delayed.**
4. We asked them to be quiet, but they went on **talking and disturbing us.**

5. You have to take driving lessons if you want to learn **to drive a car.**
6. The boxes were so heavy that I couldn't manage **to carry them upstairs.**
7. My favorite teacher in school used to encourage us **to ask questions when we didn't understand something.**
8. I'm sorry, I forgot **to mail that letter you gave me.**

Follow-up

Ask the class to compose sentences using these verbs from part A that didn't come up in parts B or C: *enjoy, choose, hope, intend, promise, allow, teach.*

13.4   I prefer . . .

Warm-up *(1–2 minutes)*

Books are closed. Ask the class to tell you some of the things they *hate doing / hate to do.* Tell them some of the things you like and hate. For example:

*I like to drive a car – but I hate being a
    passenger.*
I love eating good food – but I don't like to cook.

Procedure

A   Books are open. Have everyone study the verbs in the list for a few moments. Answer any questions. This exercise can be done by students working alone.

ANSWERS
1. **She loves to play / playing golf.**
2. **We were at the beach when it started to rain / raining.**
3. **He hates to take / taking showers.**

4. **She began to feel / feeling better after taking her medicine.**
5. **I don't know if I want to continue to study / studying math next year.**

Point out that although we can say both "I like to play tennis" and "I like playing tennis," only *to . . .* can be used with *would like,* as in these examples:

Would you like to play tennis?
I'd like to play tennis with you.
I'd like you to play tennis with me.

B   *Group work*   Divide the class into groups of 4 or 5 for this discussion activity. List the verbs students are to use on the board: *love, like, hate, enjoy, dislike.* Circulate around the class and listen for relevant errors. At the end, ask two or three students from different groups to tell the class a few of the preferences they heard.

Follow-up

1. Highlight the items in the Student's Book that the class found difficult.
2. Now, to help students remember what they've learned in this unit, go through each of the items you have highlighted and have the class call out the correct form. For example, if you want to practice the verb *speak English:*

Teacher: *I enjoy . . .*
Class: *SPEAKING ENGLISH!*
Teacher: *It's easy . . .*
Class: *TO SPEAK ENGLISH!*
Teacher: *Thank you very much for . . .*
Class: *SPEAKING ENGLISH!*

Or, *buy a car:*

Teacher: *I can't afford . . .*
Class: *TO BUY A CAR.*
Teacher: *Therefore, I've put off . . .*
Class: *BUYING A CAR.*
Teacher: *But next year I hope . . .*
Class: *TO BUY A CAR.*

14 | *Doing or to do? – II*

Grammar summary

Practice in using verbs that are followed by the preposition *to* + *-ing.:*

I'm **looking forward to** see**ing** you.
I've **gotten used to** be**ing** alone.

Using *stop* + *-ing* and *stop* + *to . . .* with different meanings:

*He's stopped cough**ing** and sneez**ing**.*   (his cold is better now)
*They stopped **to** look at the map.*   (they stopped in order to look at the map)

Using *remember* and *forget* followed by *-ing* or *to . . .* with different meanings:

*I remember see**ing** her at the party.*   (it is still in my memory)
*I remembered **to** lock the door.*   (I didn't forget to do it)

Using *let* and *make* followed by an object + the base form, while *allow* and *force* are followed by an object + *to . . . :*

*Please **let me see** the photos.*
*We aren't **allowed to park** here.*
*They **made him confess.***
*They **forced him to confess.***

Relevant errors

✗ Please stop to annoying me.
✗ I'm used to work at home.
✗ I'm looking forward to go there.
✗ I forgot doing my homework.
✗ We aren't allowed talking during the exam.
✗ They made me to do it.
✗ They won't let me doing it.
✗ It stopped to rain after lunch.

14.1   Looking forward to . . .

Warm-up *(5–6 minutes)*

Books are closed. Tell the class about a few things you're going to do soon – and say if you're looking forward to doing them (have a positive attitude about them) or not looking forward to doing them (feel negatively about them). Then ask students to say what they're looking forward to doing – and what they're not looking forward to. For example:

I'm looking forward to going to the park this weekend.
I'm not looking forward to doing my laundry tonight.

Procedure

Books are open. Have students look at the illustration. What is the woman not looking forward to? For example:

She's not looking forward to getting up early.
She's not looking forward to going to classes in the morning.

A   *Group work*   Divide the class into groups of 3 or 4. Explain that each group will be discussing a friend who is about to start taking English classes. They should answer the four questions listed. Join in briefly with any group that is having trouble getting started and perhaps mention some topics in each category. For example:

looking forward to: communicating in a new language, doing fun activities in class

not looking forward to: speaking in front of the class, doing lots of homework assignments
get used to: speaking only English in class, learning grammar rules
object to: doing homework

NOTE: Some students may be confused by the use of *to* in these examples because it is really a preposition (which is followed by *-ing*), not part of the infinitive. Students may also have difficulty distinguishing between *I used to work* . . . (= I once worked, but don't anymore) and *I got used to working* . . . (= I became accustomed to working . . .). Explain these points if they come up.

B   Students should work alone as they write down their group's five best ideas. Encourage them to use *look forward to, get used to,* and *object to.* Then they should compare their sentences with the other members of the group. For example:

She's looking forward to communicating in a new language.
She's not looking forward to speaking in front of the class, but I hope she soon gets used to it.
She'll find it hard to get used to speaking English in class.
She might object to doing homework, but she'll still have to do it.

If the class needs reinforcement at the end of the exercise, dictate the preceding example sentences. Then have students read the sentences back to you to write on the board for checking.

Follow-up

Describe this situation to the class and ask students to discuss what they'd say about their friends using *looking forward to, get used to,* and *object to:*

Two American (or Canadian, Australian, British or other nationalities) friends are going to live in your country for a year. You have told them about life in your country. What are they looking forward to and not looking forward to?

What will they find hard to get used to? What might they object to?

After the discussion, ask groups to report back to the rest of the class.

14.2   Communication activity: Stop!

Warm-up *(4–6 minutes)*

Books are closed. Tell the class: "Everyone stand up for a follow-the-instructions game." (It isn't actually necessary to stand to do the activity, but standing seems to set the right mood.) "You must do as I say. If even one student can do it, the class gets a point. If no one can do it, I get a point."

Read the instructions one by one, allowing time for "acting" after each. Be sure that everyone sees or hears you (or a student) clearly demonstrate each instruction before you call out another one.

INSTRUCTIONS

sigh	whisper to yourself
whistle	sniff
tap your pen	clear your throat
stare at me	click your tongue
stare at the door	blink both eyes fast five times
hum a tune	tap your foot

Procedure

Books are open. Have students look at the examples and the illustration in the Student's Book and ask them to work out the difference in meaning implied by the use of *stop* + *-ing* or *stop* + *to* . . .

Pair work   Divide the class into pairs. Student A should look at Activity 10, and Student B at 17. The activity is in two parts.

As this is a slightly complicated activity, you should spend a little time explaining to the class how it works: "**Part One**   In the first part, you will be practicing the use of *stop + -ing* and *not + -ing* by asking each other to stop doing various annoying things, like whistling and tapping your foot. For example: *Please stop tapping your foot. Would you mind not whistling?*

"**Part Two** In the second part, you will be telling each other a story about a walk you remember and explaining why you stopped from time to time during the walk, using *stop + to . . .* For example: *I had a stone in my shoe, so I stopped to take it out. It started to rain, so I stopped to have a cup of coffee at a cafe.*"

Have students read the instructions in Activities 10 and 17 carefully before they begin their conversations. Answer any questions about the vocabulary.

Follow-up

A   Have students write down two examples of sentences they used in the first part and two examples of sentences they used in the second part of the activity.

B   Have students describe a long drive or trip and the stops they made along the way (or a long project and the interruptions they had), using *stop + to . . .* This can be prepared in pairs before the students tell their story to the class. The drive, trip, or project could be real or imaginary.

14.3   Communication activity: Don't forget!

Warm-up *(5–6 minutes)*

Books are closed. Put the following pairs of sentences on the board and talk about them:

I forgot to put the key under the mat.   (I intended to put the key there, but I didn't.)
I forgot putting the key under the mat.   (I put the key under the mat, but I didn't remember that I had done it.)
I remembered to call the restaurant.   (I didn't forget – I called the restaurant.)

I remember calling the restaurant.   (I recall that I called the restaurant.)

Procedure

Books are open. Have students look at the examples and the illustration in the Student's Book. Ask them to work out the differences in meaning implied by the use of *remember + -ing, remember + to . . ., forget + -ing,* and *forget + to . . .*

Pair work   Divide the class into pairs: Student A looks at Activity 16, and Student B at 26. This is similar to the activity for Exercise 14.2. Take time to explain how the two parts work, and perhaps write the two pattern conversations on the board: "**Part One** In the first part, you will be practicing the use of *remember + to . . .* and *forget + to . . .* by asking about some things on a shopping list. For example, Student A will ask: 'Did you remember to do the shopping?' And Student B will reply: 'Yes, I remembered to do the shopping. Did you remember to mail the letter?'

"**Part Two** In the second part, you will be telling each other about some happy memories, using *I remember + -ing* and *I'll never forget + -ing.* For example, Student B will ask: 'What do you remember about a vacation you enjoyed?' And Student A will reply: 'I remember going on vacation to the coast for the first time when I was a child. I'll never forget seeing the ocean.'"

Make sure students read the instructions in Activities 16 and 26 carefully before they begin their conversations. Answer any questions about vocabulary.

Follow-up

Ask the class to talk about some things they actually forgot / didn't remember to do recently. Ask them to think back to this time last week, and ask:

What do you remember doing in your English class?
What do you remember doing before and after the class?

14.4   Rules

Warm-up *(2–3 minutes)*

Ask the class to look at the "Keep off the Grass" sign and the sentences to the left of it. Then look at the list of expressions at the bottom of the exercise. Elicit other ways of making sentences about this rule, using some of these expressions. For example:

Sitting / Walking on the grass isn't allowed.
We have to stay off the grass.
They make us keep off the grass.

Procedure

This can be done by students working together in pairs, or working alone and then comparing sentences in pairs. Tell them they should write at least six sentences, using each of the phrases shown. For example:

We aren't allowed to smoke.
Singing and dancing aren't allowed.
They make us show respect to the teachers.
They won't let us arrive later than 8:55.
We have to speak only in English.
Writing in ink is required.
Silence is required when the teacher is talking.
We have to do two hours of homework every
  night.

Follow-up

1. Tell students to imagine that they are unfortunate enough to be students at the school whose rules are shown in the Student's Book. Ask them to say how they feel, using the phrases given. For example:

I wish they'd let us sing.

It's too bad we can't shout.
I'm glad they don't allow cheating.

2. Ask the class which rules they think are too strict and which they think are OK. You may be surprised at their responses!
3. Have students make up some "class rules" for their own class that would help everyone to learn and practice English effectively.

14.5   In other words . . .

Warm-up

Begin by asking students to spend a few moments looking through the previous exercises in Units 13 and 14. Answer any questions that arise about the uses of *-ing* and *to* . . .

Procedure

This is a review exercise that can be done for homework or in class.

ANSWERS
1. Please stop **asking so many questions.**
2. We aren't allowed **to park on school grounds.**
3. I'm not used **to meeting strangers.**
4. I forgot **to tell you my phone number.**
5. **Eating** too much ice cream **makes me feel sick.**

Follow-up

Ask the class to look through this unit and the previous one again (preferably at home) to see if they understand everything or if they still have questions. Have them write sentences to help them to remember some of the more difficult points.

Grammar summary

Practice in using prepositions of place:

> in   on   at   behind   in front of
> beside   next to   between   among
> below   underneath   on top of   inside
> outside   near   a long way from
> across

The missing wallet was **underneath** a pile of books **behind** my desk.

Using prepositional phrases to describe exact positions:

> on / to the left of   on / to the right of   on
> the left-hand side of   on the side of   on
> the edge of   on the other side of   in the
> corner of   at / on the corner of   at the
> top of   at the bottom of   in the middle of
> at the back of   at the front of

It's **in the corner of** the room **on the left-hand side of** my desk.

My house is **on / at the corner of** First and Maple Streets.

Using prepositions of motion and direction:

They ran **through** the field and jumped **over** the fence.

Are you going **past** the post office on your way **back from** the bank?

Relevant errors

✗ It's in middle of the room.
✗ It's on left of the house.
✗ She's sitting at a chair.
✗ It's among the two trees.
✗ It's in front the door.

Other errors include using prepositions or prepositional phrases imprecisely or in a misleading way.

15.1   Mouse trouble

Warm-up *(1–2 minutes)*

Books are closed. Ask for a volunteer to help you illustrate some prepositions. Give the student an object (e.g., a book or a bag – something large enough to be visible). Then ask him or her to place the object:

> on the desk
> in front of the desk
> in the middle of the desk
> next to / beside the desk
> on the edge of the desk
> in the corner of the desk
> underneath the desk
> to the left of the desk

Ask for suggestions from the class if the volunteer needs help.

Procedure

Books are open. Begin by showing how the position of each mouse in the illustration can be identified. For example:

There's one underneath the sofa.
There's one on top of Mr. Brown's head.

Have students look at the illustration while you describe the positions of a few mice; ask students to raise their hands when they have found the particular mouse you're describing.

This exercise can be done as a whole class. Students should draw a circle around each mouse in their books – but they must not do this until its position has been described *precisely* by someone in the class. Seeing the mice is easier than describing where they are, and students may need help with suitable language while they're doing this.

Follow-up

A *Class work*   When all the mice have been located (there are 30 mice altogether) and their positions described, tell the class exactly where you want them to put three mousetraps – and to mark the location of each one with an "M." For example:

Put the first mousetrap underneath the bed, next to the wall below the window.

Then have members of the class tell everyone else where they want more mousetraps to be placed. Again, they should mark the spot with an "M."

B Describe the following diagram to the class step by step, and have them draw the details as you say them. *Don't* tell anyone what the diagram represents.

INSTRUCTIONS
"First of all, draw a large square. Inside the square, filling most of the area, draw an oval or egg shape. Draw a wavy line along the bottom half of the oval. Draw two half-circles on the left and right of the oval, both outside it, with their

points touching the edge of the oval. Now draw two straight lines joining the top of the oval to the square. Now draw a very small circle in the middle of the oval, and two larger circles side by side below that. Join those two circles with a straight line. Draw two more straight lines, joining the two circles to the edges of the oval. Put a dot inside each of the circles. Finally, draw a half circle between the tiny circle in the middle and the top of the oval – its points should be pointing downwards.

"Now turn your paper upside down and compare your drawing with your partner's!"

Refer to every item as a line, dot, or circle – *not* as a nose, eyes, or ears! Allow questions at any stage in case you haven't made yourself clear. Students may want to know what you mean by "a large square" or "a very small circle," for example, so you may need to give approximate dimensions in inches or centimeters.

This activity is quite a challenge!

15.2   In the mountains

Warm-up *(2–3 minutes)*

Books are open, but students shouldn't write anything. Go through the first part of the story, asking the class to suggest what word or words could fill the blanks. Make it clear that *more than one word* can be used to fill in the blanks, and that sometimes several different answers are possible.

You can make the activity more enjoyable by miming parts of the story as you tell it. Pause for the class to suggest what word or words come next. For example:

There I was, standing alone . . . [you stand up, perhaps on a chair] *on the top of the mountain looking . . .* [you mime looking at a wonderful view, shading your eyes] *at the view. I could see the sun starting to set . . .* [you point to the sun as it starts to set] *in the west. Slowly a red glow spread . . .* [your arm sweeps across the horizon] *across / over the sky, until the sun finally went . . .* [you point again to the sun going right down out of sight] *down.*

Tell and mime the rest of the story in the following Follow-up.

Procedure

Pair work   Divide the class into pairs or groups of 3. Students should do the exercise together, discussing any problems that arise. Point out that in some cases, more than one answer is possible – and that they can fill some of the blanks with a phrase, not just a single word.

SAMPLE ANSWERS
There I was, standing alone **at the top of / on the top of / on** the mountain looking **at** the view. I could see the sun starting to set **in** the west. Slowly a red glow spread **across / over / through** the sky, until the sun finally went **down**. I could see gray clouds **in** the sky and could feel a chill **in** the air. Soon it would be very dark. I started to walk **down** the slope **to / toward / in the direction of** the mountain hotel. I was going to spend the night **there**. I walked slowly, because the path was covered **with** snow and ice. Suddenly it began to snow heavily. I stopped **beside / under / beneath** a tree and watched the flakes come **down**. I didn't want to get lost in the dark, so I walked on **in / through** the snow.
  At last I saw the hotel **in front of / ahead of / before** me. By the time I reached it, I was very cold and wet. Once I was **inside,** however, I soon began to warm up. I sat **beside / next to / in front of** the fire, drinking hot chocolate and singing songs **with** my friends.

Follow-up

Books are closed. Go through the whole story once more with the class, telling and miming the story (see the preceding warm-up). Pause before each missing preposition and ask the students to supply the missing words. (If you don't feel comfortable miming, tell the story in the same way but without the actions.)

15.3   Where is my . . . ?

Warm-up *(8–10 minutes)*

Books are closed.

1. Bring some office supplies and other odds and ends into class, preferably including some of the things mentioned in the Student's Book:

coffee cup	pencil sharpener	calculator
address book	paper clips	
cassette player	scissors	
box of airmail envelopes	pen	stapler
notebook	dictionary	

2. Arrange the things in a disorganized fashion around the room. Now ask the class to tell you where each item is – without pointing to it and without touching it. For example:

Teacher: *Where's my notebook?*
Student: *It's on the window sill, underneath your dictionary.*

Procedure

Pair work   Books are open. Divide the class into pairs. Students should begin by looking again at the phrases listed in Exercise 15.1. Tell them how long they have to do this exercise, so that they know how long their turn will be. (Each turn lasts about 2–3 minutes; the warm-up and follow-up will take a lot more time.)
  First, Student A asks Student B to describe the location of some items. Then tell everyone to switch roles. Now Student B asks Student A to describe the location of some other items.

Follow-up

Class work   You'll need 20 to 30 paper clips for this activity.

1. Count the paper clips so that you and the class know how many there are.
2. Give the paper clips to two students and tell them to hide them anywhere they like in the classroom. While they do this the rest of the class should watch, but *you* should turn your back or close your eyes. To help themselves remember, students may want to take notes while this is being done (e.g., *on the window sill, under John's books,* etc.).
3. Ask the class to tell you exactly where each paper clip is. Count each one as you find it until you have them all. If any are missing, ask the students who hid them to tell you where they are.

15.4   Communication activity: Go straight until . . .

Procedure

Draw the top left-hand part of the diagram (from page 31 in the Student's Book) on the board.

```
  1    2    3    4    5    6
 11   12   13   14   15   16
 21   22   23   24   25   26
 31   32   33   34   35   36
 41   42   43   44   45   46
 51   52   53   54   55   56
```

Then demonstrate the kind of thing the students will have to do in this activity by explaining this "route" while you're drawing it on the board:

"First of all I'm going to draw two spots or blobs, like the one that's over 38 in your book.

One is between 22 and 23 and the other is between 23 and 24.

"Now I'm going to draw a line, starting between 31 and 32, going upwards between 21 and 22 and 11 and 12 and curving around above 2 and then curving down below 13, and going up again to make a curve above 4. Now it goes straight down between 14 and 15 and stops between 34 and 35.

"Now I'm going to draw a small circle around number 33."

NOTE: This is a very challenging activity, which is both useful and enjoyable. It shouldn't be done too quickly – allow plenty of time.

Pair work   Divide the class into pairs. Student A looks at Activity 18, and Student B at 45. A third student can share A's task and information. Make sure no one "cheats" by looking at the wrong activity. Pencils, not pens, should be used so that mistakes can be erased. If you wish, you may photocopy the diagram on page 31 in the Student's Book for students to write on.

Each student describes a "route" between, around, past, over, to the left of, or to the right of the numbers in the diagram. The route becomes a picture, but everyone should concentrate on drawing the lines according to the instructions. They aren't expected to produce an artistic piece of work.

The students describing the route should watch what the others are doing and tell them if they make a mistake – but they must tell them, not point or show them.

While everyone is doing this, go around helping students to describe some of the more difficult movements. Make sure both partners have a turn – you may need to interrupt before Student A has finished if time is running short.

Follow-up

Have everyone secretly draw a simple line drawing (a cat and dog, a house and some trees, or something like that). Then, working in pairs or in small groups, each person explains to the other(s) how to draw the same picture.

16 | *Prepositions – II*

Grammar summary

Describing routes:

> *Turn left at . . .   Turn right at . . .*
> *Go straight.   When you get to the . . .*
> *When you've passed the . . .*

Using adjectives that are usually followed by *about* or *of:*

> *angry about   happy about*
> *nervous about   etc.*
> *afraid of   terrified of   scared of*
> *proud of   etc.*

I'm worried **about** *the future.*
She's scared **of** *flying.*

Using adjectives that are usually followed by *at:*

> *good at   great at   terrible at*
> *better at   etc.*

He's pretty good **at** *tennis and even better* **at** *volleyball.*

Using adjectives that are followed by particular prepositions:

> *interested in   polite to   different from*
> *responsible for   sorry for   etc.*

I'm interested **in** *baseball.*
I feel sorry **for** *people with no home.*

Relevant errors

✗ He's good in baseball
✗ She's interested for golf.
✗ Turn on the left.
✗ I feel sorry with them.

And any other incorrect uses of prepositions.

16.1   This way, please!

Warm-up *(2–5 minutes)*

Books are closed. Ask the class to name some cities in Canada (e.g., Ottawa, Quebec, Toronto, Montreal, Vancouver). If possible, locate Toronto on a map of Canada. Have students who know something about Toronto tell the others. If you have visited Toronto or know anything about it, tell the class.

Procedure

Books are open. Have everyone look at the map of Toronto. To remind the class how to give directions, explain a simple route using the map, from City Hall to Union Station by way of St. James' Cathedral, for example. (Have everyone find City Hall and start there, but don't tell the class where you are going. Give the series of directions and then ask the class where they have arrived.)

A *Pair work*   Divide the class into an *even* number of pairs, with a couple of groups of 3 if necessary. It will help with this activity for students to have a pen and a pencil (or different color pens) at their disposal – one for marking their own route, and the other for marking another pair's route later. If you wish, you may photocopy the map and distribute a copy to each student.

Make it clear that this is a walking tour and that the shortest route possible will be the least exhausting for the tourists.

B   Form groups of 4 by combining pairs. Allow time for both pairs to get a turn at

playing the roles of "tour guides" and
"tourists."

Follow-up

1. Use a large map of the city your students are
studying in. Choose as a class the "top ten"
tourist attractions in the city.
2. Now divide the class into groups and have
them work out an interesting walking tour of
the city – starting and ending at your classroom.
3. Ask the groups to present their tour to the
whole class, or to another group.

16.2   How do you feel?

Warm-up *(1–2 minutes)*

Books are closed. Write on the board:

I get / am angry about . . .
I get / am worried about . . .
I'm afraid of . . .

Tell the class one or two ways to complete each
sentence about yourself (e.g., *I get angry about
not getting a bigger raise. I'm worried about my
uncle's health. I'm afraid of going to the dentist.*)
Tell students that in a few minutes they'll have
a chance to give their own answers (in part B).

Procedure

Begin by going through the adjectives shown in
part A: Make sure everyone knows what they
mean. If anyone is unsure what a word means,
act out its meaning (or ask for a volunteer to act
it out).

A   This can be done by students together in
pairs, or working alone. There are many
possible answers, and students working in pairs
may have different ideas about appropriate
answers. Encourage them to talk about their
opinions.

NOTE: Students may come across some of
the adjectives in part A followed by different
prepositions. For example: *delighted by, happy
with, heart-broken over, glad of.*

The actors were delighted by the applause.
I'm not happy with my new car.
She was heart-broken over the death of her pet.
I was glad of having a chance to thank them.

SAMPLE ANSWERS
She's **delighted / glad / happy / pleased about**
   getting the job.
He's **nervous / upset / worried about** tomorrow's
   exam.
She's **nervous / upset / worried about** going out
   alone at night. OR She's **afraid / frightened /
   scared / terrified of** going out alone at night.
He's **angry / annoyed / furious / upset about**
   being kept waiting.
She's **annoyed / depressed / disappointed /
   upset about** missing the show.
He's **heart-broken / sad / upset about** leaving his
   girlfriend.

B   *Pair work*   Students should work in
pairs or groups of 3 for this open-ended
discussion activity. It may be necessary to make
sure students are sensitive to each other's
feelings and don't "pry." (If you like, you can
give everyone the option of responding twice
during the exercise with, "I think I'd rather not
answer that one.")

Follow-up

With a more advanced class, point out that this
exercise includes only a few of hundreds of
similar adjective + preposition combinations.
Ask students to suggest some more and write
them on the board. For example: *fond of, aware
of, allergic to, similar to.* Then have students
make up sentences using them. For example:

He is very fond of his dog.
Are you aware of the rules about smoking?
She says she is allergic to cats.
Your car is similar to mine.

16.3   Are you good at math?

Warm-up (*4–5 minutes*)

Books are closed. Tell the class: "We're going to play a memory game. I'm going to tell you three sentences about my neighbor Pat when she was a child. I'll repeat the sentences three times while you listen. Then I'll give you a minute to write down the three sentences from memory. Ready?" Use these patterns:

She was better at math than she was at reading.
She used to be more interested in climbing trees
    than in doing her homework.
She wasn't as good at schoolwork as she was at
    sports.

After the writing period, let students compare papers if they wish. Then have the class read you the sentences to write on the board for checking.

Procedure

Books are open. The exercise introduces some adjectives + preposition combinations that students often find confusing. If you think your students will find this very hard, go through the exercise first, making sure they know what prepositions to add. However, at this stage they shouldn't write anything down. Explain any vocabulary that's unfamiliar.

A   This exercise can be done in pairs, or by students working alone and then comparing sentences in pairs later.

SAMPLE ANSWERS
2. But I'm afraid I was pretty bad **at basketball and other sports.**
3. Since graduating from school she has gotten very interested **in environmental issues.**

4. He is very proud **of what he has achieved.**
5. Life in my country is quite different **from life in Canada.**
6. Foreigners who visit my country are always impressed **by how polite and friendly everyone is.**
7. By the time we arrived, the room was full **of people / smoke.**
8. I always try to be polite **to everyone – especially to strangers.**
9. I didn't know you were studying. I'm sorry **for interrupting you.**

B   *Pair work*   Divide the class into an even number of pairs for the first part of the activity. For the second part of the activity, form groups of four by combining pairs.

Follow-up

1. Highlight the items in the Student's Book that the class found difficult in this unit.
2. Now, to help everyone remember what they've learned in the unit, go through each of the items you have highlighted and have the students write sentences using the correct preposition. The sentences should be *true* sentences about themselves. For example:

interested: *I'm very interested in soccer.*
afraid: *I'm not afraid of spiders and*
         snakes.
thrilled: *I was thrilled about being invited to*
         the party.

Form pairs or groups of 3. Have students ask each other *why* they have written each sentence. For example:

Why are you interested in soccer?
– *Because it's a very exciting sport and I used to*
   play it at school.
Why aren't you afraid of spiders or snakes?
– *Because most of them are harmless.*

There is more practice on using prepositions in Unit 19: Verbs + Prepositions.

17 The future

Grammar summary

Practice in using different forms to talk about future events and activities:

You**'ll** *get cold if you don't wear a coat.*	– PREDICTION
I'm going to *apply for a new job.*	– INTENTION
*She***'s going to** *have a baby.*	– CERTAINTY about a future event, based on situation now
I'm seeing *the dentist tomorrow.*	– ARRANGEMENT
Their train **arrives** *at 8:00.*	– TIMETABLE
I'll *pay you tomorrow.*	– PROMISE
I won't *forget our appointment.*	– PROMISE
I'll *open the door for you.*	– OFFER
Will *you let me know soon, please?*	– REQUEST
Shall *we stop here for lunch?*	– SUGGESTION

Using the present simple or present perfect in a time clause or an *If . . .* clause, instead of *will* and *going to:*

I'll have lunch **when** *they* **arrive.**
We'll go out **if** *it* **doesn't rain.**

NOTE: The following sentences all convey the same information, but each has a slightly different meaning:

I'm going to visit New York on the 12th.
I'll visit New York on the 12th.
I'm visiting New York on the 12th.
I visit New York on the 12th.

However, for intermediate students, these differences may not matter very much.

Relevant errors

✗ I'll wait here until the bus will arrive.
✗ Everything is getting better soon.
✗ The weather gets better next week.
✗ If I'll pass my exam, I'll be happy.
✗ If I'm going to pass my exam, I'm going to be happy.

17.1 One day . . .

Warm-up *(5–10 minutes)*

Books are closed. Write *superstitious* and *superstitions* on the board and ask the class:

Are you superstitious?
Do you believe in superstitions?

Then write on the board:

If you . . . , you'll have good / bad luck.

Ask the class to tell you some common superstitions by completing the sentence. For example: *If a black cat crosses in front of you, you'll have bad luck. If you find a rabbit's foot, you'll have good luck.* You may uncover some interesting differences and similarities in superstitions, especially in a multinational class.

Help students formulate grammatically correct sentences. Point out the use of the simple present in the *If . . .* clause. Then change the sentences on the board to read:

You'll have good / bad luck if . . .

Using this sentence pattern, have the class recall and repeat all the superstitions that have been mentioned.

Procedure

Spend some time looking at each of the cartoons and the words in the speech balloons. Make sure everyone understands what the captions mean (INTENTION, ARRANGEMENT, etc.). Ask students to think of additional examples for each caption.

Have students practice the pronunciation of "gonna," the reduced form of "going to." If anyone is uncomfortable using the reduced form, however, don't force it.

A *Pair work*   Divide the class into an even number of pairs. Go around the class helping out as necessary.

SAMPLE ANSWERS

2. One of these days, if I have enough money, **I'm going to take a trip to the Caribbean.**
3. By the time the bus **arrives / gets here,** we'll all be soaking wet.
4. This weekend, if the weather's good, **I'm going to go camping.**
5. After this class is over, we**'re going to go for a pizza.**
6. Their plane **takes off / leaves / lands / arrives** at 6:05 tomorrow morning.
7. As soon as I can, **I'll let you know my new address.**
8. **I won't** tell anyone about our little secret.
9. Look out! That big black dog **is going to bite / attack you!**
10. Since it's our teacher's birthday tomorrow, we**'re going to invite her to / out for lunch.**

B   Form groups of 4 by combining pairs, and have students compare sentences. Point out that it's often possible to use *going to* and *will* interchangeably – for example, *I'll let you know my address* (PROMISE or OFFER) has a similar meaning to *I'm going to let you know my address* (INTENTION).

C *Pair work*   First, write these incorrect sentences on the board (or choose some similar quotes from work that students have done recently), and ask the class to say how each one should be rewritten correctly (the correct sentences appear in parentheses):

By the time the bus will arrive, we'll all be soaking wet.   (By the time the bus arrives, we'll all be soaking wet.)
The dog will bite you if you won't be careful.   (The dog will bite you if you aren't careful.)
What are you going to do this evening if the weather will be nice?   (What are you going to do this evening if the weather is nice?)

Divide the class into pairs. Make sure everyone finds all the errors and corrects them. Check the answers as a class.

ANSWERS
(Errors are underlined and correct sample sentences follow.)

1. I'll make some coffee when my friends <u>will arrive</u>.
   I'll make some coffee when my friends arrive.
2. I think <u>I go</u> out for a walk soon.
   I think I'll go out for a walk soon.
3. If <u>they're going to have</u> enough money, they're going abroad this summer.
   If they have enough money, they're going abroad this summer.
4. We won't catch the train if we <u>won't hurry</u>.
   We won't catch the train if we don't hurry.
5. Her sister-in-law <u>has</u> a baby next month.
   Her sister-in-law is going to have a baby next month.

Follow-up

This activity gives more practice in using time clauses. It also introduces different adverb phrases that are used to refer to future time. First, write *if, when, while,* and *as soon as* on the board. Then tell the class that you're thinking of visiting a number of different countries and cities in the near future, and that you and they are going to talk about them, using the words on the board.

Choose countries and cities that your students know something about – either places in their own country or places they've seen in movies or have actually visited. For example, if your students are Japanese, or know about Japan, your conversation might go like this:

Teacher: *I'm thinking of going to Kyoto one of these days.*

Student A: *If you go there, I bet you'll visit lots of temples.*

Student B: *While you're there, you'll probably visit Kiyomizu Temple.*

Student C: *When you go there, will you have time to go to Nara?*

Student D: *If you're in Kyoto, will you stay in a Japanese-style inn?*

Student E: *If you're there in the autumn, the trees will be beautiful.*

Student F: *As soon as you arrive, will you take a nap or go sightseeing?*

(If the class needs help getting started, you could read this conversation to give them an example of what you want them to do.)

Here are some other ways you might begin in order to introduce different adverb phrases that refer to future time:

I might go to .... sooner or later.
I'm probably going to .... the year after next.
I thought I might go to .... one day soon.
I'm thinking of going to .... in a year or two.
I was wondering about going to .... in a few months' time.
I'm off to .... next week.
I'd like to go to .... one of these days.
I plan to go to .... in a few years' time.
I really want to visit .... sometime during my life.

17.2   Consequences

Procedure

Go through the first couple of "threats," asking the class to say how they'd react. For example:

Teacher: *I'm going to drink two whole liters of milk. (OR quarts / cartons of milk)*

Students: *If you drink two liters of milk you'll be sick.*
If you drink two liters of milk there won't be any left for breakfast.
If you drink two liters of milk you'll regret it.

Group work   Divide the class into groups of 3 or 4. Have students take turns role-playing the part of the "friend" while the others react. Encourage everyone to think of various possible consequences of each statement.

SAMPLE REACTIONS
1. **If you drink two whole liters of milk, you'll make yourself sick.**
2. **If you drive too fast, you'll have an accident.**
3. **If you hold your breath for ten minutes, you'll turn blue and faint.**
4. **If you don't phone home this month, your parents will be upset.**
5. **If you steal that old woman's purse, you'll never be able to forgive yourself.**
6. **If you never come to this class again, we'll all miss you.**
7. **If you keep studying until your English is perfect, you won't have time to do anything else.**

At the end, ask each group to choose two of their reactions and tell them to the class.

Follow-up

Have the class, working in pairs, write down some more similar threats. Then they announce them to the rest of the class, who have to react. For example:

I'm not going to do any more homework!
If you don't do any more homework, you won't make much progress.
If you don't do any homework, you'll get into trouble.

17.3   Planning ahead

Warm-up *(2–3 minutes)*

Have the class ask you about some of your plans for next week, perhaps day by day. Then tell them how those plans will change if you're sick. For example:

On Monday night I'm going to a concert. If I'm sick I'll give my ticket to a friend.

Procedure

A   Students work alone. Encourage students with few plans and appointments to invent some imaginary plans so that their calendars are full. NOTE: Although *p.m.* can refer to both afternoon and evening, for the purposes of this exercise it refers to afternoon; therefore, students fill in their plans on the calendar for morning (before noon), afternoon, and evening.

B   *Pair work*   Students find out what their partner is going to do each day. Then they find out how unexpected events might jeopardize their partner's plans. For example:

A: *What are you going to do on Monday morning?*
B: *I'm going to go to work.*
A: *What will you do if you're sick on Monday morning?*
B: *If I'm sick I won't be able to go to work. I'll have to stay in bed. What are you going to do on Saturday afternoon?*
B: *I'm going to play tennis.*
B: *What will you do if the weather's bad?*
A: *If the weather's bad, I won't be able to play tennis – I guess I'll stay home and watch TV.*

To end the practice, call on two or three pairs to "perform" one of their conversations for the class.

Follow-up

Have each student find out from his or her partner what the most interesting or exciting thing is that she or he is planning to do next month.

Then students tell the rest of the class what their partner is going to do, and the other students ask how the plans might change if something unexpected happens. For example:

First student: *My partner says she's going to fly to Hawaii next month!*
Another student: *What if there's an air traffic controller's strike?*
First student: *Well, if there's a strike, I guess she'll have to wait for the first available flight.*

17.4   Next summer . . .

Warm-up (*2 minutes*)

Books are closed. Tell the class about all the things you're planning to do during your next vacation. Use your imagination, if you have no plans.

Procedure

A   Books are open. This can be done in class (by students working in pairs or alone) or as homework.

SAMPLE ANSWERS
Next summer I**'m going to** have a really great vacation. Of course, I**'ll** have to save up for it and go without some luxuries, because otherwise I **won't be** able to afford it. I haven't decided where I**'m going to** go yet. On the one hand it **would / might be** nice to go somewhere warm and sunny where I**'ll be able to / can** lie on the beach all day. On the other hand I **may / might** get bored with that, so it **might / may be** better to choose a more active vacation. The important thing **is to** have a real change from routine. While I**'m** away, I**'ll** send you a postcard!

B   *Group work*   This should be done in groups of 3 or 4. Encourage everyone to give details, not just a short sentence. For example:

I'm going to stay with my uncle on his farm, and most of the time I'll have to help with the work there. But I guess I'll have some time to myself, and then I'll be able to . . .

This activity could be extended as a written composition.

Follow-up

1. Divide the class into an even number of pairs. Tell the pairs that they have won a "dream vacation" together. They get to choose where they will go and what they will do, all expenses paid. Allow enough time for them to discuss this and make notes of their itinerary.

2. Then form groups of four by combining pairs, and have students tell each other what they're going to do on their vacation, starting like this: "When we go on vacation we're going to . . ."

3. End the exercise by quickly asking all the pairs for one sentence about where they are going to go, so that the whole class can enjoy hearing about the various destinations.

18 | *Possibility and probability*

Grammar summary

Practice in talking about probability and improbability:

It'll probably *rain.*
It probably won't *rain.*
It looks as if it'll *rain.*
It doesn't look as if it'll *rain.*
It's likely to *rain.*
It's not likely to *rain.*

Talking about certainty and impossibility:

I'm *absolutely* **sure it'll** *rain.*
I'm *absolutely* **sure it won't** *rain.*
It's sure to *rain.*
It won't *rain,* **that's for sure.**

Talking about possibility and uncertainty:

It may *rain.*
There's a chance it'll *rain.*
It **might** *rain.*
It **could** *rain.*

Judging the truth of statements:

It's probably *true.*
It could be *true.*
It sounds as if it's *true.*
It can't be *true.*
It must be *true.*

Judging the likelihood of past events:

It probably *happened.*
It can't have *happened.*
It might have *happened.*
It could have *happened.*

Relevant errors

✗ It might happen yesterday.
✗ It might probably rain.
✗ It must be happen.

✗ I'm sure it might not rain.
✗ It seems to be not going to happen.
✗ It may be rain.
✗ It might to rain.

18.1 Communication activity: Is it true?
Procedure

Elicit two or three statements from the class about the photograph, encouraging the use of the modal verbs given in part A. For example: *It might be whipped cream. It could be a whirlpool in the ocean. It can't be anything that's alive!*

A *Group work* Divide the class into groups of three to talk about the picture. After a few minutes, ask groups to report their ideas back to the class. Did anyone guess what the photo actually shows? (The photograph shows the eye, or center, of a hurricane.)

B Keep the class in groups of three. Student A should look at Activity 6, Student B at 24, and Student C at 30. Each student has seven statements that may or may not be true. The idea is to find out the others' opinions by asking them: "Do you think it's true that . . . ?"

Encourage students to use the structures listed in part A on page 36 of the Student's Book during their conversations. They should also discuss their reasons for believing or not believing the information given.

At the end – but not until the end – you can reveal that all the odd-numbered statements are true and the even-numbered ones are false.

ANSWERS
The incorrect information in these even-numbered sentences is <u>underlined</u>, and the correct information is given in *italics*.

Activity 6

2. More babies are born on <u>Sunday</u> in the United States than on any other day of the week.   *Not true. In fact, more babies are born on Tuesday.*
4. Mirrors absorb <u>20%</u> of light on each reflection.   *Not true. They absorb 10%.*
6. People can only distinguish <u>three</u> tastes.   *Not true. They can distinguish four tastes: sweetness, sourness, saltiness, and bitterness.*

Activity 24

2. Your nose and ears don't stop growing <u>till you are 40</u>.   *Not true. They continue growing all your life.*
4. On a clear <u>moonlit</u> night, a person on a mountain peak can see a match struck 50 miles away.   *Not true. It has to be a completely moonless night.*
6. If you get wet and cold, you are more likely to catch a cold.   *Not true. You may feel sick and miserable but you can only catch a cold from another person: It's an infection.*

Activity 30

2. The feet of a housefly are <u>10</u> times more sensitive to sugar than a person's tongue.   *Not true. Their feet are 10 million times more sensitive.*
4. In New York City the rats outnumber the people by <u>2 to 1</u>.   *Not true. The ratio is 9 to 1.*
6. People who smoke cigarettes have <u>10%</u> more motor vehicle accidents than nonsmokers.   *Not true. They have 40% more accidents.*

Continue the discussion with the class if you or the students find it hard to believe some of the preceding information or the odd-numbered sentences (which are true).

Follow-up

Divide the class into an even number of pairs. Have them write down five things about themselves that are *true* and five things that are *untrue* (but that could be true). Tell them to mix up the true and untrue statements so the statements aren't in any special order.

Form groups of four (pairs of pairs). Each pair asks the other pair to discuss which statements they think are true. For example:

Student A: *B's parents both have red hair.*
Student C: *That could be true, don't you think, D?*
Student D: *No it can't be true. B's hair is very dark.*
Student B: *You're right, D. They both have dark hair like me.*

18.2   How sure are you?

Procedure

A   Give the class a minute or so to look over the examples. Then ask everyone to speculate about the likelihood of various different types of weather tomorrow, using expressions from part A:

> *thunderstorm   sunny weather   very hot*
> *very cold   shower   snow   frost*
> *cloudy weather   typhoon   tornado*
> *strong wind   etc.*

For example:

Teacher: *I think it might snow tomorrow.*
Students: *No, I don't think so. It's not likely to snow. / Oh, I think it'll probably snow. / No way! It won't snow, that's for sure.*

Then ask about the likelihood of various real events happening in the near future. For example:

Is this very cold weather going to continue till the weekend?
Which team is going to win the game tonight?
Will the parade this weekend cause a traffic jam?

Make sure everyone studies these examples before beginning part B.

B   *Pair work*   Divide the class into an even number of pairs. Students should write down their answers to the questions after discussing them. Point out that they should write complete sentences, not just "yes" or "no"!

C   Rearrange the class into groups of 4 (pairs of pairs) for students to compare ideas. At the end, you can take a poll to see how the different groups answered the questions.

D   *Group work*   Students should remain in groups of 4 for this discussion. Before they start, go through the expressions in part A again, considering how the expressions are used if you're talking about yourself. For example:

I'm sure that I'll be rich and famous.
I'll probably be rich and famous.
I don't think I'll be rich and famous.
I'm not going to be rich and famous, that's for sure.

Then have the groups look at the illustrations in the Student's Book and ask them to say how likely it is that each of the scenarios shown represents their own future. For example:

Do you think you'll ever be like the person in the first picture?
- *No, I'm not likely to be a vice-president.*
- *Well, in ten years I want to be president of a company.*

Do you think you'll ever get married and have a big family?
- *Eventually I'll probably get married, but I only want one or two children.*
What about you?
- *I'm sure that it'll happen. I want lots of children!*

Do you think you'll ever be a teacher, like the man in the third picture?
- *It's not likely to happen – my grades are terrible.*
- *I may become a teacher in a few years, but for now I want to travel.*

Do you think you'll ever have the time to spend all day at the beach?
- *No, I don't think it'll happen. I plan to work forever.*
- *Yes. In fact in a few more years I'll probably retire and spend all my free time at the beach.*

Follow-up

Use a set of large photos from magazines. Hold each one up for everyone to see, and ask the class to work in pairs as they speculate what is likely to happen next, using the expressions in part A.

One member of each pair should play the role of "optimist" and the other the role of "pessimist." For example, if your photo shows someone on a mountain, students might say:

Pessimist: *He might fall and kill himself. Or there may be a snowstorm and he might freeze to death.*
Optimist: *Oh no, I don't think he'll fall. And it's not likely to snow. I'm sure he'll make it back safely.*

Allow everyone to change roles half-way.

If you can't find photos that are large enough for the whole class to see very well at once, pass around smaller photos. Have pairs write down their optimistic and pessimistic speculations, switching roles half-way. Then hold up each photo, which everyone has already seen up close, and ask students to read their ideas for everyone to hear.

18.3   What might have happened?

Warm-up *(3–4 minutes)*

Use the same photos you used in the follow-up for Exercise 18.2. Have the class talk about what events may have preceded the scene shown in the photograph. Alternatively, have students look back at the cartoons accompanying Exercise 18.2, part D, and speculate what might have happened before each one. For example:

She might have been a secretary who got promoted.
She could have changed jobs recently.

Procedure

A *Pair work*   Divide the class into pairs. Make sure students discuss what might have happened in each cartoon *and* decide what is likely to happen next. Mention that if we are quite sure about something we can say:

He must have been in an accident.   (= I'm sure he was in an accident.)
He can't have been in an accident.   (= I'm sure he wasn't in an accident.)

B   Students should write down their ten best ideas from the discussion in part A. This can be done in class or as homework.

Follow-up

A   Have everyone write a paragraph that is the *middle* of a story. This story could be about a memorable day, a terrible journey, or an interesting experience – or the story of a movie, perhaps.

Form groups of 3 or 4. Each student shows her or his work to others in the group, who then speculate what might have happened first and what happened next. For example:

You probably left home late. You might have been delayed. You must have left something at home.

Ask the groups that finish faster than the others to write down their speculations and/or to choose one of their story pieces to read to the whole class for speculation.

B   This activity reviews the whole unit. Read each of these sentences to the students and have them rewrite each one with the same meaning. They should begin their sentences with the words given on the right – write these on the board.

1. I'm sure our train will be late.   *Our train* ....
2. I probably won't see you tomorrow.   *I don't* ....
3. No one told me about the party.   *I'm* ....
4. I'm sure they are a very happy couple.   *They* ....
5. She'll be promoted, that's for sure.   *She's* ....
6. This definitely isn't your handwriting.   *This* ....

SAMPLE ANSWERS
1. Our train **will probably be late / is sure to be late.**
2. I don't **think I'll see you tomorrow.**
3. I'm **sure no one told me about the party.**
4. They **must be a very happy couple.**
5. She's **sure to be promoted.**
6. This **can't (possibly) be your handwriting.**

19 | *Verbs + prepositions*

Grammar summary

Practice in using verbs that are followed by different prepositions with different meanings:

> *look for* (try to find)   *look after* (take care of)   *look at* (observe)
> *I'm looking **for** my shopping list.*
> *She looked **at** me as if I were crazy.*

Using verbs that are followed by a particular preposition:

> *stare at   welcome someone to*
> *introduce someone to someone else   share*
> *something with someone   etc.*
> *He shared his Coke **with** her.*
> *I couldn't help staring **at** them.*

Using verbs that are followed by different prepositions before "someone" or "something":

> *argue with someone about something*
> *speak to / with someone about something*
> *apologize to someone for doing something*
> *etc.*
> *He **apologized** to her **for** breaking the glasses.*

Relevant errors

✗ I'm looking after my pen – I can't find it.
✗ Please don't laugh to me.
✗ Look after me while I'm talking to you.

NOTE: Because of the nature of the grammar involved, this unit is less "active" than previous ones. Nevertheless, the exercises will be communicative if students do them in pairs in class. The follow-up activities provide further communicative practice.

For a change of pace, however, you may prefer to have students do most of the exercises as homework – many students like the chance to take their time and focus on accuracy.

19.1   Add the prepositions

Warm-up (*5–6 minutes*)

Books are closed. Introduce the unit by giving the class a few examples of "verbs + preposition." First, write *stare* on the board and ask students to demonstrate what it means. Next write, *Why are you staring* .... *me?* and ask the class to choose the correct preposition according to the situation that you are going to read to them.

Situation 1: A father who is in the kitchen cooking dinner says to his daughter: "Where's the baby? I don't hear him. Can you look .... him?" (for; *look for* = try to find)

Situation 2: A mother says to a friend who is a nurse: "My baby isn't feeling well. Can you look .... her?" (at; *look at* = observe)

Situation 3: A father says to his mother: "I have to go to the dentist, and I need someone to watch the baby. Can you look .... her for about an hour?" (after; *look after* = take care of)

Point out that *look* can be followed by different prepositions with different meanings.

Procedure

Books are open. Have students look at the illustrations and talk about what they show. For example:

She's looking for something.
She can't find her keys.
She's wearing them around her neck.

NOTE: If you anticipate that your students will find this exercise very difficult to do, start by reading the whole exercise aloud, asking them to suggest what prepositions fit in each blank. But they should *not* write anything at this stage.

A This can be done in pairs in class, treating it as a sort of problem-solving task. In this way students can get valuable practice in communicating while they're discussing the exercise. Alternatively, it can be done as homework if time is short.

ANSWERS
1. I've looked everywhere **for** my keys.
2. Who's going to look **after** the business while you're away?
3. She tends to feel embarrassed when people look **at** her.
4. Don't you know it's rude to stare **at** people?
5. I'll never forgive them **for** what they said to me.
6. I think you should apologize **for** what you have done.
7. He threw the ball **to** his friend, who caught it easily.
8. They were so mad they started throwing plates **at** each other.
9. Afterwards they were able to laugh **about** the incident.
10. We asked **for** the check after our meal.
11. Don't laugh **at** her or she'll get angry.
12. He gets very upset if someone shouts **at** him.
13. Those plaid pants don't go **with** your striped shirt.
14. I don't have my dictionary because I lent it **to** a friend.
15. They borrowed $8,000 **from** the bank to buy a new car.
16. How much did you pay **for** the meal?
17. Thank you very much **for** helping me.
18. Welcome **to** Puerto Rico! I hope you enjoy your stay.
19. I'd like to speak **with / to** you **about** your work.
20. He didn't say anything **to** me **about** his plans.
21. I disagreed **with** him **about** what he should do.
22. She talked **with / to** him **about** the book she'd read.
23. He argued **with** her **about** her point of view.
24. I'm going to discuss it **with** them tomorrow.
25. I dreamed **about / of** prehistoric monsters last night.
26. What part of Canada do you come **from?**
27. She's thinking **about / of** changing her job soon.
28. I was just thinking **about** how to solve this problem.
29. I was hungry, so she shared her sandwiches **with** me.
30. We were all looking forward **to** having dinner together.

B This can be done by students working alone or together in pairs. Have students highlight *ten* of the verbs + prepositions combinations they found hardest to remember (or any ten difficult ones). Make sure everyone sees another student's (or pair's) sentences at the end.

Follow-up

Divide the class into pairs. Have everyone test each other like this: One student closes her or his book while the other reads the beginning of each sentence. The other has to say what comes next. For example:

Student A: *It's your turn first: "I've looked everywhere . . ."*
Student B: *"for my keys."*
Student A: *Right. "He gets upset if someone shouts . . ."*
Student B: *"to him." No, sorry I mean: "at him."*
Student A: *OK.*

The student who answers doesn't have to remember exactly the same words as in the Student's Book. In fact, anything that makes sense is acceptable. Have students switch roles after every six sentences.

19.2   Rearrange the sentences

Procedure

Pair work   Divide the class into pairs; tell them that there may be several possible arrangements of the beginnings and ends of the sentences.

POSSIBLE ANSWERS
1. Everyone praised him **for** doing so well on the exam.
2. This house reminds me **of** a place I used to visit.
3. We congratulated her **on** her performance in the concert.
4. I can't forgive him **for** being so rude to me. OR I can't forgive him **for** telling lies and cheating on the exam.
5. She tried to blame us **for** her own stupidity.
6. They named their daughter **after** their favorite movie star.
7. He punished his son **for** telling lies and cheating on the exam. OR He punished his son **for** being so rude to me.

Follow-up

1. Divide the class into an even number of pairs.
2. Have them think of some more sentences containing verbs + prepositions that they find challenging (possibly from Exercise 19.1, part B).
3. They should fold a piece of paper in half vertically and write the beginning of each sentence on the left and the ending on the right, but *omitting* the preposition.
4. They tear the paper down the fold and then cut the left-hand and right-hand pieces into separate strips.
5. They pass the strips to another pair, who have to arrange them appropriately and add the missing prepositions.

19.3   Fill in the blanks

Warm-up (*2–4 minutes*)

Books are closed.

1. Write on the board: *The teacher praised the class* .... *speaking only English.* Elicit (or suggest, if necessary) *for* and write it in the blank. Then erase *speaking only English,* leaving *The teacher praised the class for* .... Ask the class for ways to finish the sentence. For example: *being patient, their patience, their excellent papers,* etc.
2. Erase *praised* and write in *advised.* Ask the class what word must be changed as a result of changing the verb. Replace *for* with *to* so that the board reads: *The teacher advised the class to* .... Ask for ways to finish the sentence. For example: *study hard for the next test, hand in their homework on time, speak English all the time,* etc.

Procedure

Books are open. If a lot of the prepositions here are "new" to your class, go through the exercise asking students to suggest what prepositions fit in each blank. They should *not* write anything at this stage.

When students are ready, they can do the exercise in pairs in class, or as homework. They should write their sentences on a separate sheet of paper.

ANSWERS
2. It was easy to see **through** his disguise.
3. Young Billy takes **after** his father, Bill.
4. Maria looks **like** her mother, doesn't she?
5. I don't feel **like** going out for lunch today.
6. She's working **on** a new book about James Dean.
7. Those yellow shoes don't go **with** your green pants.
8. Driving after you've been drinking is asking **for** trouble.

9. They spent a week in the capital and then headed **for** the country.
10. The University of Hawaii sounds **like** a good school. I'm going to send **for** some information.
11. The letters TOEFL stand **for** Test of English as a Foreign Language.

Follow-up

Divide the class into pairs. Have everyone test each other like this: One student closes her or his book while the other reads the beginning of each sentence. The other has to make up a continuation for each sentence – or remember the continuation in the exercise. For example:

Student A: *"It's hard for me . . ."*
Student B: *"to get used to foreign food."*
Student A: *Right. "Maria looks . . ."*
Student B: *"for her mother." No, in this case: "like her mother."*

19.4   Use your own ideas . . .

Warm-up (*3 minutes*)

If necessary, go through the exercise asking the class to say what prepositions are missing. They should not write them down at this stage, but should rely on their memories later.

Procedure

A *Pair work*   Divide the class into an even number of pairs. Encourage students to use their own ideas to make interesting sentences, and to avoid writing *for them* or *into it* all the time.

SAMPLE ANSWERS
3. He wasn't paying attention and crashed **into a parked car.**
4. I have to stay home tonight and prepare **for my classes tomorrow.**
5. All the furniture in the room belongs **to my roommate.**
6. Whether or not we go out depends **on the weather.**
7. There was so much noise that I couldn't concentrate **on what I was trying to do.**
8. In my opinion, an ideal breakfast consists **of juice, fruit, and cereal.**
9. It was an awful hotel and we complained **about the poor service and the dirty room.**
10. We only had one sandwich, so it was divided **between us / into four pieces.**

B   Form groups of four (pairs of pairs) for everyone to compare ideas. Students should also check each other's work for errors.

C   This can be done as homework, to save time in class.

Follow-up

Divide the class into two teams. The members of each team have to supply a sentence using a verb + preposition from this unit. For example:

Teacher: *Team A. Your word is complain.*
Member of Team A: *They complained about the service in the restaurant.*
Teacher: *Good, 1 point. Team B: laugh.*
Member of Team B: *Everyone laughed at him.*

Each team gets one point every time they supply a correct sentence.

Grammar summary

Using phrasal verbs formed with a verb of motion + a "particle":

> VERBS: *jump, run, come, climb, drive, pull, push, bring, go, etc.*
> PARTICLES: *up, down, in, out, past, away, back, off, over, etc.*

The general saluted as the soldiers **marched past.**

Please **go away** *and don't* **come back.**

My dog **ran away** *and we can't find him.*

Using idiomatic phrasal verbs, where it's not possible to work out the meaning from its parts:

I can't **make out** *what they're saying.* (I can't hear them / understand them clearly.)

My brother and I don't **get along.** (We aren't good friends.)

We **checked in** *early for our flight.* (We arrived early at the airport and showed our tickets.)

Using phrasal verbs that are not followed by an object (notice the correct word order):

The plane **took off** *on time.*
> but not: *The plane took on time off.*

Roses **come out** *in the summer.*
> but not: *Roses come in the summer out.*

Let's **get together** *next week.*
> but not: *Let's get next week together.*

Using phrasal verbs that are followed by an object, with the correct word order:

Please **take** *this soup* **away.**
Please **take away** *this soup.*
Please **take** *it* **away.**
> but not: *Please take away it.*

She **turned** *the radio* **on.**
She **turned on** *the radio.*
She **turned** *it* **on.**
> but not: *She turned on it.*

NOTE: In some cases a verb + preposition (*take after, look like, stare at,* etc.) may look like a phrasal verb. But notice the word order in these examples.

Ann **takes after** *her father.*
> but not: *Ann takes her father after.*

Ann **takes after** *him.*
> but not: *Ann takes him after.*

Tom **looks like** *his mother.*
> but not: *Tom looks his mother like.*

Tom **looks like** *her.*
> but not: *Tom looks her like.*

Relevant errors

✗ The plane took on time off.
✗ Roses come in the summer out.
✗ Let's get next week together.
✗ Please take away it.
✗ She turned on it.
✗ Jane takes her father after.
✗ She takes him after.
✗ Tom looks his mother like.
✗ He looks her like.

NOTE: Like Unit 19, this is not a particularly active unit. Remind students that if the exercises are done in pairs in class, valuable communication will be taking place between partners as they discuss their answers to the questions. Nevertheless, you may wish to have students do some of the exercises for homework and discuss them later in class.

20.1 We couldn't get down

Warm-up (*5–10 minutes*)

Books are closed. This exercise is intended to reassure students that many phrasal verbs have an easily understood, literal meaning.

Take a supply of suitable objects to class (e.g., a box, briefcase, or other container; a small toy with wheels; a hat or belt; a cup; a ball; a coat hanger; a stapler; a kitchen timer; a letter in an envelope).

Write the following verbs + particles on the board:

bring back / here   take away / out   pull out
push around   put in   carry over

Then put the objects in different places in the classroom. Ask the class to tell you what to do with them next, using phrasal verbs. For example, you place a cup on the desk in front of a student, who may then say: "Take it away. Now bring it back. Put it in the box. Now take it out. Now push it around . . ." etc.

If necessary, remind students of the difference between *bring* (movement toward the speaker) and *take* (movement away from the speaker).

Procedure

A   Books are open. Look at the lists and elicit from the class which combinations of verbs and particles are more likely than others. The idea is for students to work out the meaning of the phrasal verbs as they combine words.

NOTE: Many of the phrasal verbs listed in the sample answers have idiomatic as well as literal meanings. If a student suggests a verb + particle combination that doesn't have a literal meaning, ask the student to use it in a sentence to check that everyone understands. For example, for the phrasal verb *bring off* (meaning "accomplish"), an appropriate sentence would be: *I brought off my class presentation without any problems.* With more advanced students who have experience with phrasal verbs, you may want to focus more on idiomatic than literal meanings by giving sentences and asking students to supply the meaning of the phrasal verb. For example:

I'd like to bring up *another point.* (= mention).
All this homework is getting me down. (= depressing me)
The company decided to pull out *of the business deal.* (= withdraw from)

SAMPLE ANSWERS
bring **around / back / by / down / in / out / over / up**
carry **around / away / in / out / over / past / up**
climb **around / down / in / on / out / over / past / up**
come **around / away / back / by / down / in / out / over / up**
drive **(can be used with all the particles listed)**
fall **away / back / by/ down / in / off / on / out / over**
get **(can be used with all the particles listed)**
go **(can be used with all the particles listed)**
jump **around / away / back / down / in / off / on / out / over / up**
pull **away / back / down / in / off / out / up**
push **(can be used with all the particles listed)**
ride **around / away / back / by**
run **(can be used with all the particles listed)**
take **away / back / down / in / off / on / out / over / up**
walk **(can be used with all the particles listed)**

B   Students can work in pairs and complete the sentences either orally or in writing. Afterwards discuss the answers as a class.

SAMPLE ANSWERS
3. She was standing in my way and I couldn't **get past / by.**
4. The fence was too high for them to **climb / jump over.**
5. When you've finished with my books please bring them **back.**
6. I realized that I was lost and was **walking / driving / riding / running around** in circles.
7. His finger was stuck in the bottle and he couldn't **get / pull** it **out.**
8. Please **take off** your muddy boots before you come inside.

Follow-up

Divide the class into pairs and have them write more sentences (maybe six, or more if there's time) using other phrasal verbs from the list in part A. Have them show another pair what they have written.

20.2   Word order

Warm-up *(3–5 minutes)*

Books are closed. Write this dialogue on the board:

A: *Let's call up Mary.*
B: *OK. Look up the number, pick up the receiver, listen for the dial tone, dial the . . .*
A: *I know! Cut out the noise!*
B: *Hey! Why did you put down the receiver?*
A: *It was busy!*

With the help of the class, underline the phrasal verbs: *call up, look up, pick up, cut out* (meaning "stop it / stop talking"), *put down*. Don't underline *listen for*, which is a verb + preposition (see Unit 19). Show how the word order of the underlined phrasal verbs can be changed by reading through the dialogue using the alternate word order (e.g., *call Mary up; look the number up; pick the receiver up; cut the noise out; put the receiver down*).

Have a pair of students read the dialogue aloud, changing the word order. Have another pair of students read it, leaving A's part as written and changing the order in B's part. Then have A's part reversed and B's read as written. Finally, erase the particles *(up, down, out)* and have students supply the missing words as they read and/or use a "disappearing dialogue" technique by erasing bigger and bigger chunks until the students are saying the dialogue with virtually no clues.

Procedure

Books are open. Look at the examples as a class, and encourage students to rely on their "feeling" for what sounds right or wrong.

NOTE: With more advanced students, you may want to identify verbs + prepositions in the following examples from the Student's Book (i.e., *ran down;* see Unit 19). The phrasal verbs (verb + particle) are denoted with an asterisk (*). The others are verb + preposition.

He wrote down* the address.
He wrote the address down*.
He wrote it down*.
~~He wrote down it.~~
She ran down the hill.
~~She ran the hill down.~~
~~She ran it down.~~
She ran down it.

Some more examples for more advanced students:

She's going out.*   (an intransitive phrasal verb, i.e., without an object)
She's putting on her hat.*
She's putting her hat on.*
She's putting it on.*
but not: *She's putting on it.*

She's looking in the box. (verb + particle)
   but not: *She's looking the box in.*
She's looking in it.
   but not: *She's looking it in.*

The exercise should be done by students together in pairs. Encourage them to discuss the task as they work.

ANSWERS
2. ~~They opened up them.~~
   They opened up their presents.
3. It's hard work bringing up children.
   ~~It's hard work bringing up them.~~
4. ~~The car drove the bridge over.~~
   The car drove over the bridge.
5. ~~She walked it past.~~
   She walked past it.
6. I'm working on my science project.
   ~~I'm working it on.~~
7. He took off his coat.
   ~~He took off it.~~
8. Your socks don't go with those pants.
   ~~Your socks don't go them with.~~
9. Flowers come out in the spring.
   ~~Flowers come in the spring out.~~

Follow-up

Have everyone look again at the sentences in Exercise 20.1, part B. Discuss which of them could be rephrased using pronouns. For example:

He jumped off the cliff.
He jumped off it.
   but not: *He jumped the cliff off.* OR
                  He jumped it off.

20.3   In other words . . .

Warm-up

If Exercise 20.3 contains a lot of phrasal verbs that are "new" to your students, go through the whole exercise as a class, discussing what the phrasal verbs mean and how the sentences would need to be rephrased. Students should *not* take notes at this stage.

Procedure

The exercise can be discussed in pairs in class and then written, or it can be done as homework.

SAMPLE ANSWERS
2. We **started out** early in the morning.
3. We intended to **stop over / stop off** in Honolulu.
4. There was a thunderstorm but the plane **kept on** flying.
5. But soon the pilot decided to **turn back** to Tokyo.
6. When I finally arrived at the hotel I **checked in**.
7. The elevator was **worn out**.
8. It usually **broke down** after breakfast.
9. I called a friend of mine, and we arranged to **get together** for a meal.
10. At the end of my stay I **checked out**.
11. Whenever there are games at parties I like to **join in**.
12. During the party all the lights **went out / went off**.
13. We **kept on** playing our game in the dark.
14. Suddenly there was a bang like a bomb **going off**.
15. Then all the lights **went on** again.

Follow-up

Divide the class into pairs. Have everyone test each other like this: One student closes his or her book while the other reads the beginning of each sentence. The other has to say what comes next. For example:

Student A: *"I arrived at the hotel and checked . . ."*
Student B: *"in."*
Student A: *Right. "The elevator was worn . . ."*
Student B: *"down"?*
Student A: *No: "out."*

Have partners switch roles when half the time is up.

20.4   Fill in the blanks

Warm-up

Again, if the exercise contains a lot of phrasal verbs that are "new" to your students, go through all the sentences and phrasal verbs as a class first. Discuss what the phrasal verbs mean and how the sentences would need to be rephrased. Many of the phrasal verbs in this exercise are used idiomatically, but students can use contextual clues to work out the meanings. Students should *not* take notes at this stage.

Procedure

Students should complete the sentences in writing, either in pairs in class or as homework.

ANSWERS
2. That's way too loud. Please **turn it down**.
3. Oh, the news is on. Could you **turn it up** now, please?

4. Gee, the news is so depressing, I'd like you to **turn it off**.
5. But if *you* want to hear it, go ahead and **leave it on**.
6. Last year I **gave up** my job of 10 years.
7. I don't know what **brought on** this change of heart.
8. It wasn't easy to **bring up** the topic of quitting with my boss.
9. The company had to hire someone else to **carry out** my duties.
10. I **gave away** all my possessions so I could travel.
11. I wanted to **put off / call off** my meeting with Mr. Brown.
12. So I **called up** first thing in the morning.
13. I had to wait while the operator tried to **put me through**.
14. His secretary said he was busy and asked me to **call back**.
15. I said no, and threatened to **call off** the whole deal.
16. I have this very complicated form to **fill out**.
17. I've written the wrong date so I'd better **cross it out**.
18. I can't **make out** this word – the type is too faint.
19. I don't know my grandmother's maiden name, so I'll just **make it up**.
20. I've had enough of this: Could you please **take it away**?

Follow-up

Divide the class into pairs. Tell students that they should use six of the verbs from this unit in a single paragraph. The phrasal verbs should be written in pencil, and the rest of the paragraph in ink.

When the paragraph is complete, they erase the phrasal verbs and pass the paragraph to another pair. The other pair has to fill in the blanks.

At the end, students should check their sentences with the pair who wrote them.

21 | *If . . . sentences – I*

Grammar summary

If . . . can be used in three different types of conditional sentences:

1. *If I* **see** *her, I***'ll** *tell her.*   (I may see her.)
   If I **see** *her, I* **won't** *forget to tell her.*   (I may see her.)
   If I **don't see** *her, I* **won't** *be able to tell her.* (I may not see her.)

2. *If he* **were** *more friendly, he***'d** / *he* **would** *be more popular.*   (He isn't friendly.)
   If they **were** *more friendly, we* **wouldn't** *dislike them.*   (They aren't friendly.)
   If she **weren't** *so friendly, she* **wouldn't** *be so popular.*   (She is friendly.)

3. *If I* **had known** *you won, I***'d have** / *I* **would have** *congratulated you.*   (I didn't know.)
   If I **had known** *it was a secret, I* **wouldn't have** *told anyone.*   (I didn't know.)
   If we **hadn't** *turned on the TV, we* **wouldn't have** *seen the news.*   (We did turn it on.)

Using *If . . .* or *unless . . .* + present (as type 1 above):

If I **wake up** *early, I***'ll go** *for a run.*
If I **don't wake up** *early, I* **can't go** *for a run.*
I **can't go** *for a run if I* **don't wake** *up early.*
I **won't go** *for a run unless I* **wake** *up early.*

Using *If . . .* + past (as type 2 above)*:

If he **knew** *more, he***'d** / *he* **would pass** *the exam.*
*He***'d** / *he* **would pass** *the exam if he* **knew** *more.*
If he **were** *more studious, he* **might** *pass the exam.*   (not: If he was more studious . . .)

*Although the verb in the type 2 sentences is the past form, it is the subjunctive tense. In colloquial English you might hear: *If he'd just be more friendly, he would meet more people.*

Although used conversationally, this usage is not taught or accepted in formal written English. The correct form is: *If he were more friendly, he would meet more people.*

Using *if, unless, when,* and *until* to communicate different meanings:

I'll make coffee **when** *they arrive.*   (They will arrive.)
I'll make coffee **if** *they arrive.*   (But they may not come.)
I won't make coffee **until** *they arrive.*   (Not before they come.)
I won't make coffee **unless** *they arrive.*   (But they may not come at all.)

Relevant errors

✗ I'll buy it unless I have enough money.
✗ If I would be rich, I would be happy.
✗ If I am rich, I'll buy a yacht tomorrow.
✗ If I'd be rich, I'll buy a Porsche.
✗ Life would be easier when I were rich.
✗ If I'll see him, I'll tell him.
✗ If I saw him, I'd told him.

21.1   *If, unless, when, until*

Warm-up *(4–6 minutes)*

Books are closed. Ask three to six students to help you. Assure them that you will tell them what to do, not "test" them.

1. Write on the board: *Raise your hand if you have a paper clip.* Have the helpers open their hands. Ask the class: "Should they raise their hands?" (The answer is no, because they don't have paper clips.)

99

2. Hand out paper clips to a few of the helpers so that only some of them, not all, have a paper clip. Have a student read the instruction written on the board again. Ask the class: "Should Jane raise her hand?" (Yes, because she has a paper clip.) "Should Joe raise his hand?" (No, because he doesn't have one.)

3. Now write on the board: *Raise your hand unless you have a paper clip.* If possible, elicit from the class what the helpers should do. (This time, helpers *without* paper clips raise their hands.)

4. Collect all the paper clips. Repeat: "Raise your hand unless you have a paper clip." (All helpers should raise their hands.)

5. Write on the board: *Raise your hand when you have a paper clip.* This time helpers raise their hands at the moment of receiving a paper clip.

6. Collect all the paper clips. Write on the board: *Raise your hand until you have a paper clip.* The helpers should raise their hands and then drop them when they receive a paper clip.

Procedure

Books are open. Look at the illustration and the example in the speech balloon. Ask the class to explain why *if, unless, when* and *until* are used.

The exercise can be done in pairs, so that students can share their ideas. Note that other answers are possible, as well as those given.

SAMPLE ANSWERS
2. I can't work **if** you keep interrupting.
3. Come and see me **if / when** you feel lonely.
4. We'll have coffee **when** we've finished.
5. Let's wait **until** our friends arrive.
6. I'll call you **when** I get to the airport.
7. You can't do that **unless / until** you have permission.
8. We'll go by car **unless** you want to walk.
9. Don't phone me **unless** you need my help.

Follow-up

Divide the class into an even number of pairs. Have them think of four more sentences, using *if, when, unless,* and *until.* They should write

down only the beginning of each sentence. For example: *We're going to have lunch when ...*

Next students exchange their sentences with another pair, who have to complete the sentences. Then the complete sentences are returned to the first pair so that they can compare the completions with what they had in mind. While this is going on, go around checking what the students have written and making corrections if necessary.

21.2 What are you going to do?

Warm-up (*1–2 minutes*)

Books are closed. Tell the class about some of your own firm or tentative plans for the next few days, using *if* and *unless* to show what the plans depend on. For example:

I might do some gardening tomorrow if it doesn't rain. But if it does rain / if it rains I won't be able to, so I guess I'll stay indoors and correct some papers. But I won't do that unless I have to ...

Procedure

Pair work   Books are open. Divide the class into pairs or groups of 3. Following the pattern in the conversation will help students to concentrate on the grammar here, but more adventurous students may want to use their own ideas. For example: *I might go to a concert if I can get tickets,* or *I might go to a concert if I like what's playing.*

Point out that *unless* is not usually used before a negative. A sentence like *I'm not going for a walk unless it isn't raining* would be very hard to understand.

Follow-up

Keep the same pairs or groups of 3. Have students tell their partners what their *real* plans are for the next few days – and find out from each other what these plans depend on. At the end, ask for a few volunteers to perform their exchanges for the class.

21.3   If, if, if . . .

Warm-up

Ask the class to suggest some other things the students in the cartoon might be thinking. For example:

If I pass, I'll get a good job.
If I do well, my parents will be pleased.
If I weren't so nervous, I'd be able to answer these questions.
If these questions weren't so hard, I'd be able to answer them.
If I hadn't been so lazy, I'd have studied harder.

Procedure

The exercise can be done by students working in pairs, or working alone and then comparing sentences in pairs later.

SAMPLE ANSWERS
2. If he **were** a better driver, he **wouldn't** have so many accidents.
3. If she **had driven** more carefully last night, she **wouldn't have had** an accident.
4. If the weather **is good** this weekend, we **can / will be able to** have a picnic.
5. If I **were** President, **I'd reduce** taxes.

Follow-up

Have students write three questions, each with a different type of *if . . .* sentence. For example:

Where will you go for your next vacation if you have enough money?
How would your life be different if you were a famous movie star?
What would you have said if you had arrived late for class today?

Then students pass their questions to another student, who has to write answers. (If you want, you can start this activity by dictating the preceding examples at conversational speed. Students often need practice in "hearing" all the elements in *if . . .* sentences.)

21.4   Just suppose . . .

NOTE: If students in your class are very sensitive about discussing their height or other personal aspects, you may want to avoid some of the topics in this exercise.

This is intended to be a lighthearted activity where sentences like the following are preferable:

If I were taller, I could touch the ceiling.
If I were more intelligent, I could invent a cure for the common cold.
If I were more patient, I wouldn't get so angry when I have to stand in line.

The following kinds of sentences are *not* called for: *If I weren't so short, people wouldn't despise me.* OR *If I weren't so ugly, people might like me more.*

Warm-up *(2–4 minutes)*

Begin by asking the class to suggest some answers to these questions:

How would your life be different now if you were ten years younger?
If you were one year younger?
If you were five years younger?
If you were twenty years younger? (if your students are over 20!)

Tell them how your life would be different too.

Procedure

Group work   Divide the class into groups of 3 or 4 (but read the preceding note before beginning).

Follow-up

Ask each group to write down one sentence about each idea in the activity – preferably their most amusing, surprising, or thought-provoking ideas – and then share these with the class.

21.5   First prize!

Procedure

Look at the advertisement in the Student's Book together, making sure everyone understands the vocabulary and prizes involved. Students discuss which prize they would take or how they would spend the money. Make sure they use *would* to discuss this hypothetical idea.

Group work   This can be done in groups of 4 or 5. Make it clear that students entered the contest *as a group,* so they have to decide as a group which prize they want. Make sure students give their *reasons* for choosing particular prizes.

Groups who finish quickly could also explain which prizes they would *not* want and why.

Follow-up

Ask each group to report on its decisions to the whole class. For example:

We'd take the luxury villa as first prize because then we'd be able to spend our vacations there – we could take turns staying there. The rest of the year we could rent it out to pay for our air fares to the Caribbean. If we won second prize, we'd take the cash, because we don't need a car. We'd use the $20,000 to pay our tuition for next year, and the rest we'd donate to charity. And . . .

21.6   Complete the sentences

Warm-up *(2–3 minutes)*

Books are closed. Write on the board: *If I get up late tomorrow, I'll . . .* Ask the class to suggest several ways to complete the sentence. For example: *If I get up late tomorrow, I'll miss the bus / be late for my job interview.* Then write: *Unless I get up late tomorrow, I'll . . . ,* and ask for several possible endings. For example:

Unless I get up late tomorrow, I'll finish my homework in the morning / get a lot done / take a walk before breakfast.

NOTE: Sometimes students find it helpful to think: *Unless = if not.* For example, they can "check" the meaning of *Unless I get up late tomorrow . . .* by rephrasing it as *If I don't get up late tomorrow . . .*

Procedure

Books are open. Go through the first few sentences in part A, asking the class to suggest a few ways to complete each one.

Pair work   This exercise can be done in pairs in class (preferably an even number of pairs), or it can be done as homework if there isn't time for it in class.

SAMPLE ANSWERS
1. If I get up late tomorrow, **I'll miss my first class**.
2. If it snows a lot this winter, **we can go skiing**.
3. If I lived in China, **I'd have a very different kind of life**.

4. If I have a headache tomorrow, **I'll stay in bed.**
5. If I were a nicer person, **everyone would like me.**
6. Unless you leave immediately, **I'll call the police.**
7. I won't come and see you if **you don't invite me.**
8. I wouldn't be very happy if **my team lost the soccer match.**
9. I'll take a message if **you can't call back.**
10. I'm not going out tonight unless **I get bored.**
11. I would speak better English if **I practiced more.**
12. The world would be a better place if **there were no hunger.**

Follow-up

Divide the class into groups of 3 or 4. Ask each group to plan how they would spend "The Perfect Long Weekend," assuming they have plenty of money to spend. Where would they go? What would they do?

Ask each group to explain its ideas to the rest of the class at the end. For example:

What we'd do is this: First of all we'd get seats on a flight to Hawaii. We'd stay in the best hotel, overlooking Waikiki Beach. On the first morning we'd have a wonderful breakfast of fresh tropical fruit: papayas, mangoes, pineapples . . .

22 | *If . . . sentences – II*

Grammar summary

Practice in using past conditionals (as in type 3 in Unit 21):

If they **had known** *the truth, they* **might have** *been shocked.*   (They didn't know the truth.)
If I **had known** *the price of the shoes, I* **wouldn't have** *tried them on.*   (I didn't know the price.)
I **wouldn't have** *gone to the beach if I* **had heard** *the weather forecast.*   (I didn't hear it.)

Contracting *had* and *would* to *'d* in past conditionals:

If **I had** *known* **I would have** *told you about it.*
If **I'd** *known,* **I'd have** *told you about it.*

Sometimes "mixed" conditionals can be formed:

If I **had been** *born 100 years ago, I* **wouldn't be** *here today.*
If they **weren't** *so careless, they* **wouldn't have** *made those mistakes.*

Relevant errors

✗ If I have known, I wouldn't have told him.
✗ If I would have known, I wouldn't have told him.
✗ If I had known, I hadn't told him.
✗ If I hadn't have known, I wouldn't have told him.

22.1   She didn't win

Warm-up *(2–4 minutes)*

Books are closed. Write the following phrases on the board:

be on TV
meet Jack Nicholson
wear fancy clothes
see lots of movie stars
have a great time

Tell the class: "I'm going to tell you about a dream I had the other night. I dreamed that my friend, who was a journalist, had two tickets to the National Film Awards. He invited me to go with him, but I couldn't go because I was sick. What could I have done if I hadn't been sick? What could I have done if I had gone to the film awards?" (NOTE: If appropriate, substitute the name of a famous film festival or awards ceremony that your students are familiar with, such as the Cannes Film Festival or the Academy Awards, as well as movie stars that are popular in the students' own countries.)

Write on the board: *If I had gone to the film awards, I might / could / would have . . .* Then ask the class to suggest ways of completing this sentence. They can use the phrases you have written on the board, or they can supply their own ideas. For example:

If I had gone to the awards, . . .
– I might have been on TV.
– I might have met Jack Nicholson!

- *I could have worn fancy clothes.*
- *I would have seen lots of movie stars.*
- *I would have had a great time.*

Procedure

Books are open. Ask the class to suggest a few of the things Mary could have done if she had won first prize. Correct any relevant errors.

The sentences can be written by students together in pairs, or alone. For example:

If Mary had won, she could have traveled around the world.
If Mary had won, she could have bought her mother a new car.
If Mary had won, she might have put the money in the bank.

Follow-up

In groups, have students discuss what *they* would have done if they had won the $1 million lottery prize. Then have the groups report to the class what they would have done.

22.2 What would you have done?

Procedure

For the benefit of students who don't know about the places listed in part A, begin by brainstorming suitable places to visit and different kinds of food found in each place. If no one knows what kind of food they eat in, for instance, Brazil, point out that it's OK to say "I don't know what kind of food I'd have eaten there."

A *Pair work*   Divide the class into an even number of pairs or groups of 3. Students do not have to discuss *every* country listed, and they should not discuss the country if they really *did* spend their last vacation there.

B   Form groups of 4 (pairs of pairs) for everyone to compare ideas.

SAMPLE ANSWERS

Brazil: **If I had spent my vacation in Brazil, I would have stayed in Rio. I could have gone to the beach every day, and I might have tried *acarajé* (a round cake made of bean flour that is fried).**

Australia: **If I had traveled to Australia, I would have definitely visited the Great Barrier Reef. I might have tried scuba diving. And I could have tasted a "floater," which is a meat pie floating in pea soup.**

Hawaii: **If I had visited Hawaii, I would have stayed on the island of Maui. I could have tried surfing. I would have eaten lots of fruit, like pineapples.**

Thailand: **If I had gone to Thailand, I would have visited the capital, Bangkok. I don't know exactly what I would have eaten, but I probably would have had a lot of rice.**

England: **If I had spent my vacation in England, I would have gone to London. I might have seen Buckingham Palace. I probably would have tried afternoon tea, with scones and jam.**

France: **If I had gone to France, I could have stayed in Paris. I would have visited the Eiffel Tower and the Louvre. And of course I would have gone to lots of French restaurants, because I love French cooking.**

Italy: **If I had gone to Italy, I would have visited Venice. I could have ridden in a gondola! And I would have eaten lots of pasta!**

Japan: **If I had gone to Japan, I would have stayed in Tokyo, and I might have gone to Kyoto as well. I would have visited lots of temples and gardens. I could have eaten sashimi and sushi as well.**

Korea: **If I had gone to Korea, I might have visited Seoul, but I would have stayed in Pusan, so I could be near the sea. I could have tried *shinsollo,* which is a kind of stew made of meat, vegetables, nuts, and spices.**

Spain: **If I'd gone to Spain, I would have visited Madrid. I could have gone to the Prado, and I might have seen the caves at Altamira. I would have eaten lots of paella and flan.**

Taiwan: **If I'd gone to Taiwan, I would have**

visited Taipei. I could have seen the Lungshan Temple, the Presidential Mansion, and the National Palace Museum. I would have tried Peking duck and drunk lots of jasmine tea.

Follow-up

Have everyone choose six places listed in part A that they know the most about and write one sentence about each, beginning: *If I spent my last vacation in . . .*

22.3 If I'd been there . . .

Procedure

Go through the list in the Student's Book and answer any questions about the historical events listed.

To show that there are no "correct answers" in this exercise, ask the class to suggest several other ideas, for example:

If I'd been in Belgium in 1815, I could have been in danger.

If I'd been in Belgium in 1815, I might have been killed.

If I'd been in Belgium in 1815, I'd have been pretty scared.

Pair work   Divide the class into pairs. The activity can be treated as a sentence-writing exercise, or as a more open-ended discussion.

SAMPLE ANSWERS

If I'd been in Vienna in 1791, I could have seen / heard Mozart conducting the premiere of *The Magic Flute.*

If I'd been in London in 1863, I could have ridden on the first underground railway / seen the first underground railway open.

If I'd been in Paris in 1895, I could have seen / attended the first showing of a movie to the public.

If I'd been in Kitty Hawk, North Carolina, in 1903, I could have watched Orville Wright make his first flight in an airplane.

If I'd been in Anaheim, California, in 1955, I could have gone to the opening of Disneyland.

If I'd been at Cape Kennedy, Florida, in 1969, I could have seen the first manned rocket take off for the Moon.

If I'd been in Seoul, South Korea, in 1988, I could have seen the Olympic Games.

If I'd been in Berlin in 1989, I could have seen the opening of the Berlin Wall.

Follow-up

Divide the class into pairs. Ask them to think of some historic events connected with their *own* country and write sentences about those. Students who like sports might want to concentrate on historic sporting events, rather than political ones. Later they should show their sentences to another pair.

22.4 What if . . . ?

Warm-up (*1–3 minutes*)

Books are closed. Ask the class to suggest how they'd answer this question: *How would your life have been different so far if you'd been born in a different country?* (Choose a country that your students know about, but *not* the United States, because it is mentioned later in the exercise.)

Procedure

Group work   Books are open. If possible, divide the class into single-sex groups of 3 or 4 for this, so that everyone feels less inhibited about using their imagination. Make sure students use the structure *I would have . . .* or *I wouldn't have . . .* while they're doing the activity.

If you anticipate that the questions about being a member of the opposite sex will be too embarrassing, change the first question to: *What if you'd been born in a different era . . . ?* (for example, 100 years ago). NOTE: If any of your students were born in the United States, change the name of the country in the question: *What if you'd been born in the United States?*

SAMPLE ANSWER

If I had been born a boy, my life might have been very different in some ways. For example, I would have had a chance to play more team sports at school. I might have become a successful athlete. If I'd been a boy, my two sisters would have an older brother instead of an older sister. We probably wouldn't do as many things together, like shopping and going to the movies, so my life would have been pretty different.

Follow-up

Ask each group to report back to the rest of the class on its most amusing or thought-provoking ideas.

22.5   In other words . . .

Warm-up

Look at the first sentence and ask the class to say how the same idea could be expressed differently. For example:

If we had gone to bed at a reasonable hour, we wouldn't be so tired this morning.
We wouldn't feel so tired now if we'd had some sleep last night.
We'd feel OK this morning if we hadn't stayed up all night.

Procedure

There are many possible variations to the suggested answers. Discuss these with the class.

SAMPLE ANSWERS

2. **If he had been able to answer the questions, he would have passed the exam.**
3. **If I had seen you there, I'd have said hello.**

4. **If I could afford it, I would have been to Hawaii. OR If I could have afforded it, I might have been to Hawaii.**
5. **If the weather had been good, they would have gone to the beach.**
6. **If she had studied English before, she wouldn't be in an introductory class.**
7. **If I hadn't been so busy, I would have phoned you.**
8. **If two of our players hadn't been injured, they wouldn't have won the game.**

Follow-up

Tell the class about an imaginary journey or vacation where everything went wrong and where you made all the wrong decisions. Have them tell you what you should have done, using past conditionals. For example:

Teacher: *I bought the cheapest air ticket to New York – it was the "red-eye," and I didn't get any sleep at all.*
Students: *If you'd paid a little more you could have flown during the day. If you'd paid full fare you could have gotten a good night's sleep.*
Teacher: *When I got to New York I took a taxi to my hotel – it cost a fortune.*
Students: *If you'd taken the bus . . .*

22.6   Three paragraphs

Warm-up

Brainstorm ideas on how to complete each of the paragraphs. Make sure the meaning of each paragraph is clear to the students and that they're aware of the correct tenses to use. For example:

If I had lots of money, I'd move to a bigger apartment. I might buy a new car – I think I'd buy a sports car. I'd have a house near the ocean too, and I'd . . .

If the weather's nice this weekend, I'll go to the park. I might take some sandwiches, or buy a

*snack from a vendor and eat it outdoors. I'll
probably arrange to meet some friends and we'll
...*

*If I'd worked harder at school, I'd have done
better in my exams. I might have gotten a better
job and I'd have ...*

Procedure

Writing the paragraphs can be done for
homework to save time in class.

Follow-up

Ask students to make a short speech to the rest
of the class, telling them what they wrote for
one of the paragraphs. They should do this from
memory *without* reading their paragraphs. To
encourage the "audience" to practice listening
carefully during the speeches, have the listeners
make single notes *after* each speech: Ask them
to write the speaker's name and at least one
if... sentence they heard.

23 The passive – I

Grammar summary

This summary includes the grammar covered in Units 23 and 24.

Practice in using different forms of the passive:

Hamlet **was written** *by Shakespeare.*
  (Shakespeare wrote *Hamlet.*)
*I think I***'m being followed.**   (I think someone
  is following me.)
Being laughed at *is unpleasant.*   (It's
  unpleasant if someone laughs at you.)
He **has been arrested.**   (The police have
  arrested him.)

Using the passive to describe actions where the
person responsible is unknown or unimportant:

She **has been promoted.**   (by her boss,
  presumably)
He **was given** *a raise last month.*   (by his
  company)
I don't like **being criticized.**   (by anyone)

Transforming active sentences to the passive
and vice versa:

You have to fold the paper in the middle. → *The
  paper has to be folded in the middle.*
He was taken to the airport by his father. → *His
  father took him to the airport.*

Relevant errors

These errors are also relevant for Unit 24.

✗ My car is been stolen.
✗ My car is stealing.
✗ He was stolen his money.
✗ *Romeo and Juliet* was written from
  Shakespeare.
✗ This has written by someone else.
✗ This were written by another person.

23.1   It has to be redecorated!

Warm-up (*2–3 minutes*)

Books are closed. Tell the class about a piece of
an (imaginary) student's written work you've
been looking at: The spelling is awful, the
handwriting is terrible, it's too short, it's full of
grammatical errors, and so on. As you talk, list
these various points (spelling, handwriting, and
so on) on the board. Ask the class to say what
needs to be done. For example:

*The spelling has to be corrected. The whole
thing should be revised. An extra paragraph
needs to be written.*

Procedure

A   Books are open. As a lead-in, have the
students look at the illustration. What are Amy
and Bob doing? *(They are painting the walls.)*
Explain that this is an "active" sentence,
because we know *who* is doing the painting. Ask
if someone can rephrase that sentence in the
"passive" voice (e.g., *The walls are being
painted*). Explain that in the passive sentence,
Amy and Bob are not mentioned, so the listener
doesn't know *who* is painting the walls.

   Look at the two example sentences as a class,
and ask students to identify the active and
passive sentences. Then have them proceed by
working together in pairs, or alone.

SAMPLE ANSWERS
3. The kitchen **was finished on Monday.**
4. The bedroom **was being done on Friday.**
5. The living room **is being painted now.**
6. The walls **have been painted green.**

109

7. The ceiling **is going to be painted pink.**
8. The work **will be finished next week.**

B *Pair work*   Divide the class into pairs. First, tell everyone what you think of the decor of the classroom – the colors, the quality of the paint work, the size of the windows, the lighting, and so on. For example: *The walls have been painted a nice shade of green. The chalkboard needs to be replaced.*

If there's not much to say about your classroom, give everyone a chance to look out the window or door and talk about the rest of the building. Students can also talk about their own homes or rooms and what needs to be done there.

Follow-up

Ask for brief reports on plans for redecorating the classroom (these can be humorous!).

23.2   Communication activity: Color blind?

Warm-up *(4–10 minutes)*

Books are closed. Ask students to say what colors they might like in the various rooms of an apartment (bedroom, kitchen, living room, hall, bathroom, and so on), and which are inappropriate and why. As this is a matter of taste, students may have a wide variety of opinions, especially in a multicultural class.

Procedure

Pair work   Books are open. Student A looks at Activity 19, while Student B looks at 47. Before students start, make sure they have read the pattern conversation in the Student's Book. It may be necessary to run through the pattern together as a class first. Students should follow this pattern as they do the

activity, although once they feel more confident they can start to improvise. For example:

Student B: *The bathroom door should have been painted blue, and the walls should have been painted white. Unfortunately, the door was painted white and the walls were painted blue! The ceiling was painted tan.*
Student A: *Was that OK?*
Student B: *Yes, that was fine. But then I noticed that the front door had been painted white.*
Student A: *I think white's OK for a front door.*
Student B: *Yeah, but I wanted it to be painted gray.*

Follow-up

Ask each pair to report the worst mistake made by the painters.

23.3   Spot the errors
Warm-up

Look at the first sentence and ask the class to say what's wrong with it.

Procedure

Pair work   The exercise can be done in pairs, or by students working alone and then comparing ideas in pairs later. Before you start circulating to help students, copy the remaining five sentences on the board to use in checking the exercise.

ANSWERS

(The errors are underlined, and the correct forms are in parentheses.)

1. *Romeo and Juliet* were **(was)** written from **(by)** Shakespeare.
2. I can't give you a ride because my car is repairing **(being repaired)**.

3. I <u>were</u> **(was)** told that, after <u>been</u> **(being / it has been)** repaired, it will be as good as new. (NOTE: Students might change *will* to *would*. Although *will* is not an error, *would* is acceptable here as well.)
4. It **(is thought)** <u>thought</u> that many diseases **(are caused)** <u>caused</u> by smoking cigarettes.
5. We were <u>telling</u> **(told)** to arrive by noon, but we were <u>delay</u> **(delayed)**.
6. It was <u>announce for</u> **(announced by)** the company president that large profits had <u>be</u> **(been)** made.

Finally, make sure everyone accepts that the errors in the preceding sentences really are errors! Encourage questions.

Follow-up

Collect sentences with errors from students' oral and written work during the unit. Use some of these sentences to write a "Spot the Errors" exercise for homework or further pair work in class. Of course, change any information in the sentences that would identify the students who wrote them.

23.4   Communication activity: Has everything been done?

Warm-up *(1–3 minutes)*

Books are closed. Practice the structure *Has . . . been done?* by asking students about various class procedures. For example:

Has the board been cleaned?
Has the wastebasket been emptied?
Has the homework been collected?
Has the furniture been arranged properly?

Procedure

Pair work   Books are open. In the first part, Student A looks at Activity 7, while Student B looks at 34. In the second part, when they change roles, Student A looks at Activity 27, while Student B looks at 43. The idea is to find out what jobs have been done or not done at a garage (Activities 7 and 34) and before a party (Activities 27 and 43).

Both parts involve role-playing a phone call. If you have movable furniture in your classroom, you can make the communication more realistic by having the students sit back-to-back so that they can't see each other's faces. (In a crowded classroom this may not be feasible, however, because of noise level.)

Explain to students that this activity is in two parts, and that they'll be playing different roles in each part.

1. Before doing the first part (Activities 7 and 34), refer to the illustration and set the scene for the students: The woman has taken her car to a garage to be repaired. She is calling the garage and talking to a mechanic to see what jobs have been done.

If necessary, explain any unfamiliar vocabulary that comes up in the individual activities:

hood: the piece at the front of a car that you raise in order to work on the engine (NOTE: in some cars the engine is at the back)
windshield: the window across the front of the car that the driver looks out of
carburetor: a part of the engine where the gasoline and air are mixed
spark plugs: These are the part of the engine that ignite the gasoline and air in the cylinders
trunk: a storage compartment, usually at the back of the car, where you put luggage among other things (NOTE: in some cars the trunk is at the front)
polish: rub (usually with a cloth) to make shiny
adjust: change or regulate to make something work better

You may want to draw a picture of a car on the board; point to the car parts and mime, or explain, some of the actions involved.

Finally, before students begin, write the sample dialogue from page 47 in the Student's

Book on the board for them to refer to during the activity.

2. For the second part (Activities 27 and 43), set the scene and explain the situation: Each pair of students is giving a dinner party together. Student A has stayed home all day to prepare for the party, and Student B is calling to find out what's been done and what hasn't been done yet. You may want to write a new model sentence on the board, as it follows a slightly different pattern from the first activity:

Have you prepared the vegetables? (not: *Has anyone prepared the vegetables?*)
– *Yes, the vegetables have been prepared.*

Follow-up

Ask one or two pairs to act out one of their calls in front of the class (if possible, sitting back-to-back as if they're on the phone).

23.5 Giving instructions

Procedure

To help students with the vocabulary in part A, take a sheet of paper and demonstrate to the class how it can be folded vertically, horizontally, and diagonally to make flaps. Then show how vertical and horizontal lines can be drawn on it, dividing the paper into different size areas.

Ask students to tell you some more things to do with the paper. For example:

Please draw another vertical line down the side of the paper about five centimeters / two inches from the left-hand side.

A Begin by having students look at the example, pointing out how the passive sentences are changed to imperatives. Do the next two sentences as a class, to make sure they understand what to do.

Students can then work in pairs and rewrite the instructions in class on a separate sheet of paper. Alternatively, to save time, this could be done as homework.

SAMPLE MODEL ANSWER
Use a regular-size sheet of typing paper (8½ × 11 inches or A4) for this experiment. First of all, tear it into four smaller pieces. Do this as follows:

1. **Fold it in the middle and then tear it into two pieces.**
2. **Fold each piece again across the middle and tear it to make a total of four equal-size pieces.**

 Now place one of the pieces on the table with the long sides pointing down. Draw a horizontal line across the top of the paper about a quarter of the way from the top. Then draw two vertical lines downwards from the horizontal line, so that you divide the bottom part of the paper into three equal-size parts.

 Next, you have to tear the paper along each of these vertical lines as far as the horizontal line so that you create three flaps. Then fold the left flap toward you and fold the right flap away from you – you make the folds right at the top of the flap. You shouldn't fold the center flap, though.

 Now find a paper clip and attach this to the bottom of the center flap. Finally, raise the whole thing high and let it fall . . .

B The "experiment" creates a kind of helicopter, which rotates as it falls to the ground. Provide the class with paper clips so they can try it.

C *Group work* This activity is quite challenging, so allow ample time for it. It may be best to omit it if you only have a few minutes, or if you think it will be too difficult (or uninteresting) for your students.

Begin by looking at the illustrations of a box, a bird, a frog, and an airplane in the Student's Book. Suggest other things that can be made out of paper, such as a boat, a hat, and an envelope. Ask if anyone in the class knows how to make something out of paper, and make sure each group has one of these students in it.

As the students explain what to do, the other students in the group follow the instructions using their pieces of paper. Because students work in groups, don't insist on their using the passive all the time. Treat this as a fluency activity, where communication is more important than grammatical accuracy.

A nice thing about this activity is that it may

give shy students a chance to shine in front of their more confident classmates – it works best in groups of 3 or 4. At the end of the activity, groups can display their creations for the rest of the class.

Follow-up

A   Ask students to describe how other simple processes are carried out; for example, making a pot of tea, cooking an egg in various ways, carrying out a recipe for something. This can be done in groups or as a whole class.

B   As written homework, have students write a description of one of their ideas from Exercise 23.5, part C – either using the passive (as in the Student's Book) or the active, using the imperative or *You* . . .

24 | *The passive – II*

For Grammar Summary and Relevant Errors, see Unit 23.

24.1 Who by?

Procedure

Begin by asking members of the class to explain what some of the things in the left-hand column are. At this stage, however, they should *not* name the painter, composer, author, singer, inventor, director, or creator; let the groups work this out together later. For example:

Guernica *is a painting.*
I think radium is a radioactive chemical.
Penicillin is a kind of antibiotic drug.
Rashomon *is a movie.*
Light bulbs are used in lamps and lights.
Gone with the Wind *is a book and also a famous movie.*
A Walkman stereo is a small cassette player with earphones. You can carry it anywhere.
Mickey Mouse is a cartoon character.
"Material Girl" is a pop song, I think.
War and Peace *is a novel. In fact, it's a classic.*
This book is a textbook.
Murder on the Orient Express *is a book, and I think it's a movie too.*

Group work   Divide the class into groups of 3 or 4. The exercise can be done orally and/or in writing. Instruct students to write *complete* sentences on a separate sheet of paper.

Some groups may have to use guesswork or the process of elimination to do this exercise. Be prepared to offer some clues in case a group gets stuck.

This exercise requires the use of *appropriate verbs,* as the sample answers show.

SAMPLE ANSWERS
1. *Guernica* **was painted by Picasso.**
2. **Radium was discovered by Marie Curie.**
3. **Penicillin was discovered by Alexander Fleming.**
4. *Rashomon* **was directed by Akira Kurosawa.**
5. **Light bulbs were invented by Thomas Edison.**
6. *Gone with the Wind* **was written by Margaret Mitchell.**
7. **The Walkman stereo was invented and manufactured by Sony.**
8. **Mickey Mouse was created by Walt Disney.**
9. **"Material Girl" was sung/performed by Madonna.**
10. *War and Peace* **was written by Leo Tolstoy.**
11. **This book was published by Cambridge University Press.**
12. *Murder on the Orient Express* **was written by Agatha Christie.**

Follow-up

A   Have members of the class suggest additional famous paintings / songs / books / inventions / discoveries which were painted / sung / written / invented / discovered by people from their own country.

B   In pairs, or for homework, have students design their own lists, as in Exercise 24.1. Then they exchange their lists with another pair in class, who then have to do the task.

24.2 News headlines

Procedure

Look at the example with the class and discuss how it could be rewritten differently, using both passive and active structures. For example:

ACTIVE VOICE
Someone has stolen a valuable painting from the National Gallery.
A thief took a valuable painting from the National Gallery.

PASSIVE VOICE
A valuable painting was stolen from the National Gallery.
A valuable painting has been stolen from the National Gallery.

The exercise can be done by students working together in pairs, or working alone. Point out that although the headlines in this exercise can be rewritten using active sentences, you'd like everyone to use passive sentences. (If some students finish before others, however, you could have them write active sentences as well.)

SAMPLE ANSWERS
Over 100 people were killed on highways last month.
Over 24,000 new businesses were begun last year.
A new planet beyond Pluto has been discovered by a spacecraft.
Fifteen students were arrested after a demonstration.
The soccer championship has been won by Mexico.
The manager has been accused of accepting bribes and has been forced to resign.
A / The missing airliner has been found in the jungle, and the survivors have been rescued by helicopter.

Follow-up

Bring some copies of English-language newspapers to class and have students choose some headlines that interest them. Then ask them to rewrite them – or to simply explain them in their own words.

It doesn't matter if some of the headlines don't call for the passive – in fact, that's preferable, because it gives everyone a chance to decide when to use the passive.

24.3   Communication activity: Being . . .

Procedure

With the class, look at the illustration and examples in the Student's Book, discussing how the blanks can be filled. For example:

I hate to be criticized.
I can't stand being criticized.

I like being given presents.
Being given presents is nice.
I'd like to be given a birthday present.

Introduce some of the vocabulary from Activities 38 and 42, especially the verbs + preposition *(laugh at someone, swear at someone, sing to someone)* and the phrasal verbs *(wake someone up, tell someone off)*. For example:

I don't like being laughed at.
I hate being woken up.
I enjoy being sung to.
Being told off is upsetting. (to tell someone off means "to scold someone")

Procedure

Pair work   Student A looks at Activity 38, while Student B looks at 42. Each student has two lists of promises, threats, and offers. The idea is for students to get their partner to react appropriately, using the expressions on page 49 of the Student Book.

Explain that the activity is in four parts:

1. Student A says the things he or she is going to do (from the first column in Activity 38), and Student B reacts appropriately. For example:

Student A: *If you like, I'll send you a postcard.*
Student B: *That's great! I love being sent postcards!*

2. Student B says the things he or she wants to avoid doing (from the first column in Activity

42), and Student A reacts appropriately. For example:

Student B: *If we're not careful, someone will criticize us.*
Student A: *Oh no! I hate to be criticized.*

3. Student A says the things he or she wants to avoid doing (from the second column in Activity 38), and Student B reacts appropriately. For example:

Student A: *If we're not careful, someone will punish us.*
Student B: *How awful! Being punished is terrible.*

4. Student B says the things he or she is going to do (from the second column in Activity 42), and Student A reacts appropriately. For example:

Student B: *If you like, I'll give you a present.*
Student A: *Great! I enjoy being given presents!*

Make sure students understand the procedure before pairs start their conversation, and encourage them to use a range of expressions. More advanced students can be encouraged to use their own words, as long as they use the *being* structure.

24.4   Passive → Active → Passive

Warm-up (5–6 minutes)

1. Explain to the class that the verb *get* can sometimes be used in place of *be* in passive sentences. For example:

The trees got blown down in the storm.
His leg got broken.
She got offered a new job.

2. Make a list of disasters by brainstorming as a class, and write it on the board. Your list might include the following: *earthquake, flood, thunderstorm, volcano erupting, drought, car crash, explosion, riot, accident, war, battle.*
3. Divide the class into pairs. Ask them to write

down sentences describing one result of each of the disasters listed on the board, using *got* in their sentences. For example:

The building got damaged in the earthquake.
The driver got injured in the car crash.
Only one person got killed when the volcano erupted.
Nobody got drowned in the flood.

There are more examples of *got* in Exercise 24.4.

Procedure

Answer any questions about the vocabulary in parts A and B. Make sure students realize that they have to change the sentences from passive to active in part A and from active to passive in part B.

The two exercises can be done by students working together in pairs, or they can be assigned as homework. Discuss possible variations with the class and deal with any problems that arise.

A

SAMPLE ANSWERS
2. **Steven's father punished him.**
3. **Ann broke her leg in a skiing accident.**
4. **The wind blew down dozens of trees.**
5. **The judges awarded Karen the prize.**
6. **The mayor is going to open the new airport.**
7. **If you can't drive, who is going to drive your car?**
8. **You can't open your birthday presents until your birthday.**

B

SAMPLE ANSWERS
2. **The President was reelected.**
3. **All the witnesses are being interviewed by the police.**
4. **David's going to be given a big surprise!**
5. **My hotel room hasn't been cleaned.**
6. **I have been asked to give a talk about my country.**
7. **My car has to be fixed before I can drive it.**
8. **That movie you wanted to see is being shown this week.**

Follow-up

1. Divide the class into an even number of pairs (or groups of 3).

2. Ask the pairs to write four active sentences and four passive sentences, maybe about their own activities recently.

3. Then they should pass their sentences to another pair and ask them to rewrite sentences 1 to 4 using the passive voice, and 5 to 8 using the active.

25 Prepositional phrases – I

Grammar summary

Practice in using common preposition + noun expressions:

> in bed   in pencil
> on vacation   on purpose
> out of date   out of sight
> by heart   by accident
> at home   at school

I lay **in** *bed* **at** *home trying to learn the words* **by** *heart.*

Using prepositional phrases to describe various ways of traveling:

> for a drive   for a walk
> by car   by train
> on the train   on the bus
> in the train   in the bus
> on a trip   on a tour
> on a train   on a bus
> in a train   in a bus

Normally I come **by** *bus /* **on the** *bus, but today I came* **on** *foot.*

Relevant errors

✗ She is at bed.
✗ He said it at a loud voice.
✗ We traveled on plane.
✗ What happened on the end?
✗ She's out danger now.

25.1   In . . .

Warm-up (5–6 minutes)

This exercise introduces the overall topic of the unit. Books are closed. Ask the class: "What do you do when you're in a bad mood?" Elicit a few

answers and/or tell what you do yourself (e.g., go for a walk, listen to music, slam doors). Then dictate this paragraph (the prepositional phrases are already underlined here, but don't refer to them until after you have finished dictating):

I was <u>in a terrible mood</u> so I went <u>for a walk</u> <u>by myself</u> <u>in the rain</u>. <u>On purpose</u> I walked very fast <u>in the country</u> until I was <u>out of breath</u>. <u>At the end of my walk</u> I was <u>in a better mood</u>.

Have the class read the paragraph back to you to write on the board for checking. Then ask students, either alone or in pairs, to find and underline the ten prepositional phrases. Finish by underlining the phrases on the board.

Procedure

Books are open. Have everyone look at the list of phrases. Ask for questions on any phrases that are unfamiliar or puzzling. Then divide the class into groups and assign each group two or three lines of phrases. They should then make up sentences using some of their phrases (preferably ones they don't know so well).

Pair work   Divide the class into an even number of pairs. Make sure everyone thinks of at least two ways to complete each sentence – there are lots of different ways of completing them.

SAMPLE ANSWERS
2. I'd rather be **in a good mood** than **in a bad mood.**
   I'd rather be **in Sue's room** than **in my apartment.**
3. It's boring here indoors – let's go out **in the snow.**
   It's boring here indoors – let's go out **in a little while.**

4. I usually read the newspaper **in the evening.**
   I usually read the newspaper **in half an hour.**
5. Poor Sam! He had to spend three weeks **in the hospital.**
   Poor Sam! He had to spend three weeks **in jail.**
6. She smiled sympathetically and then spoke to me **in a kind voice.**
   She smiled sympathetically and then spoke to me **in a whisper.**
7. He's having a rough time and he's often **in tears.**
   He's having a rough time and he's often **in trouble.**
8. You can see from her expression that she's **in a terrible mood.**
   You can see from her expression that she's **in love.**
9. Such an important meeting should be held **in public.**
   Such an important meeting should be held **in the daytime.**
10. On an exam it's best to write your answers **in ink.**
    On an exam it's best to write your answers **in pencil.**

Follow-up

Form groups of 4 by combining pairs and ask the class to compare their sentences.

25.2   Going . . .

Warm-up (*2–5 minutes*)

Books are closed. Ask the class what they think is the best way to get to the following places locally (omit any that are irrelevant):

- some nearby cities or towns
- different parts of this city or town
- local beaches or swimming pools
- local places of interest
- other countries near and far

Procedure

Pair work   Books are open. This discussion activity calls for the use of much more than the phrases listed in the Student's Book – in particular, prepositions that describe direction (see Unit 16). It's quite possible to answer some of the questions without using prepositions, but encourage students to use the suggested phrases, maybe *making up* answers if necessary.

Ask pairs to report back to the class on their most interesting ideas.

SAMPLE ANSWERS
- **I got to school today by subway.**
- **Last weekend I went downtown by bus, and then I went for a run along the harbor.**
- **On my last vacation I went on a cruise. I went for a swim every day. My friends and I went on outings every time we pulled into port. Often we'd go for a walk or a drive to see the local sights. It was a great vacation, and I loved traveling by ship!**
- **To get to the top of the Empire State Building, I'd have to go by taxi to the airport. Then I'd go by plane to New York City. I'd travel by bus from the airport to Manhattan. Next I'd have to get to the Empire State Building – I'd probably go on the subway, or maybe on foot if it was close enough to walk. When I got to the Empire State Building, I'd get in the elevator and go to the top!**
- **My favorite way of traveling is on foot. I prefer walking because you have time to look at the sights around you, and because it's good exercise.**

25.3   By heart

Procedure

Go through the lists in the Student's Book and explain any unfamiliar phrases to the class.

Assign a few phrases to each group (preferably ones they don't know so well) and have them make up sentences using their phrases.

Pair work   Pairs should discuss possible endings before committing themselves in writing.

SAMPLE ANSWERS

2. We can't go to school today because **we're on vacation.**
3. The news must be true because **I heard it on the radio.**
4. I refuse to do any work at all because **I'm off duty.**
5. You can't punish them because **they didn't do it on purpose.**
6. No one likes him because **everyone thinks he's out of his mind.**
7. I'm not supposed to eat chocolate because **I'm on a diet.**
8. They weren't allowed to enter the country because **their passports were out of date.**
9. The only way to remember these phrases is **to learn them by heart.**

Follow-up

Divide the class into an even number of pairs. Ask students to pick ten phrases from the list that they didn't use in the exercise and think of sentences incorporating them. Then they should write their sentences with a blank where the relevant phrase would be.

The sentences with blanks are passed to another pair who have to fill in the blanks. Then the completed sentences are passed back to the first pair. Warn students that some of the completed sentences may be correct and suitable even if they are different from the intended answers. You may have to check some of these.

25.4   Finally . . .

Procedure

To prepare for this review section, allow a few minutes of silence for everyone to read through the lists in this unit. Students should highlight the phrases they particularly want to remember.

A   The ten sentences can be written in class, or done as homework.

B   *Pair work*   Everyone compares sentences with a partner.

Follow-up

A   To help students to remember the phrases they've learned in this unit, have them close their books. Ask them to call out all the phrases they can think of that contain each preposition. For example:

Teacher: *AT* . . .
Students: *At home! At last! At the end! At the movies!* etc.

Then do the same with *in, on, for, by,* and *out of.*

As a variation, do this exercise as a game. Students working in pairs or groups of 3 list prepositional phrases as quickly as they can. The pair or group with the longest list of correct phrases wins.

B   Ask students to make up sentences using different prepositions with the same nouns, and note the different meanings. For example:

I was at the movies yesterday.
I've never seen Arnold Schwarzenegger in a movie.
By the end of the movie, everyone had fallen asleep.

26 *Prepositional phrases – II*

Grammar summary

Practice in using prepositional phrases with *time* (see Exercise 26.1 in the Student's Book):

> *on time   in time   at the same time*
> *behind the times*   etc.
> *He never arrives* **on** *time.*
> *He arrived* **in** *time for the meal.*

Using preposition + noun + preposition expressions (see Exercise 26.2 in the Student's Book):

> *in addition to   in time for   in charge of*
> etc.
> *Sue's* **in charge of** *the office while the boss is away.*

Using prepositional phrases to connect sentences:

> *on the one hand . . . on the other hand*
> *for example   in theory*   etc.
> *I don't know what to think of this book.* **On the one hand** *it's very well written, but* **on the other hand** *it's way too long.*

Relevant errors

✗ She arrived at time.
✗ They both arrived on the same time.
✗ He's in the charge of the office.
✗ In answer of your question . . .
✗ That's right in the theory.
✗ I'm in mood for some music.
✗ On my opinion this is what we should do.

26.1   Time flies!

Warm-up *(4–6 minutes)*

Books are closed. To encourage students' interest and have a little fun, dictate this sentence:

Before my time, from time to time, my grandfather, a man behind the times who was hungry all the time, ate a whole apple pie in no time at all and at the same time drank a whole pot of coffee.

Have the class read the sentence back to you and write it on the board. Ask the class to identify and circle the subject and verb of the sentence (subject = *grandfather;* verb = *ate, drank*). Then ask students to help you rewrite the sentence *without* using the word *time.* For example:

Before I was born, my grandfather, an old-fashioned man who was always hungry, occasionally ate a whole apple pie very quickly while he drank a whole pot of coffee.

(You may want to point out to the class that the original sentence, in which *time* appears seven times, is a lighthearted example – something to repeat for fun, but not to mimic in a composition.)

Procedure

Books are open. Go through the phrases in the Student's Book and make sure everyone understands them.

on time = punctually
in time = not too late
in plenty of time = early
just in time = nearly too late
in the nick of time = at the very last moment
at the same time = together/simultaneously
before my time = before I was born or before I
    was here
at times = occasionally, sometimes
all the time = constantly
behind the times = not up to date
from time to time = occasionally
in no time at all = very quickly

Pair work   This can be done by students
working together, or by students working alone
and then comparing sentences later. Many
variations are possible.

SAMPLE ANSWERS
2. If you go by plane, **be sure to arrive at the
    airport in plenty of time.**
3. The lifeboat **saved the passengers just in
    time.**
4. Everyone should **be able to relax from time to
    time.**
5. The twins **always answer at the same time.**
6. I finished the exam **in the nick of time.**
7. If you're going to an interview, **make sure you
    arrive on time.**

Follow-up

Ask the class to suggest some more examples
using the phrases that they didn't use in the
pair work exercise.

26.2   In time for . . .

Procedure

Go through the preposition + noun +
preposition phrases and ask for questions.
Make up sentences using any unfamiliar
phrases, and have students infer the meaning.
    The sentences can be completed in pairs, or
by students working alone. Discuss any
variations that come up.

SAMPLE ANSWERS
2. Ms. Brown is the person who is **in charge of**
    this department.
3. My brother says that he's **in love with** the
    girl next door!
4. We're having a big party **in honor of** our
    parents' 50th wedding anniversary.
5. The sales manager went to the conference **in
    the hope of** getting new customers.
6. The audience started clapping and cheering
    at the end of the show.
7. I couldn't see the stage because the person
    in front of me was so tall.
8. I think I'll go out for a walk because I'm not
    in the mood for studying.
9. The magician lifted the table **with the help
    of** his two assistants.
10. The two countries are still **at war with** each
    other after all this time.
11. **In answer** to your question – I have no idea
    what the answer is.
12. They went up the Amazon in 1925 **in search
    of** El Dorado.
13. I know it's late, but am I still **in time for**
    dinner?

Follow-up

Divide the class into pairs. Ask them to write a
paragraph using four (or more?) of the phrases
listed in the Student's Book. When they have
finished they ask another pair to read and check
their work – or the paragraphs could be handed
in for you to check.

26.3   On the one hand . . .

Procedure

Begin by going through the phrases listed in the
Student's Book, giving examples where
necessary.
    This exercise gives a preview of Units 30 and
31 on joining sentences. It can be done in pairs,
or by students working alone and then
comparing answers later. Discuss any
variations that students come up with.

SAMPLE ANSWERS

1. I've thought about your proposals. Although **on the one hand** our profits will probably increase, **on the other hand** we'll all have to work harder.
2. She seemed to be asleep – **at least** her eyes were shut.
3. Ruth has some strange ideas: **According to her** / **In her opinion** / **For example,** men are inferior to women!
4. I see what you mean and **in theory** I agree with you, but I don't think your ideas will work **in practice.**
5. There are several things I don't understand; **for example,** why do I need a visa to enter the United States?
6. I sometimes have problems with reading a map – **in other words,** I usually get lost when I'm using one.
7. I know it's a big expense right now, but **in the long run** / **on the whole** it will end up saving you money.

Follow-up

Divide the class into pairs. Ask students to highlight the phrases they didn't use in the preceding exercise and then write sentences using them.

26.4   A little walk

Warm-up (*3–5 minutes*)

Books are closed. It might be fun to read this story aloud, using appropriate mimed actions and pausing for students to call out the missing words in the story. They should *not* write anything down at this stage.

Procedure

Books are open. This can be done in pairs in class, or as homework. Make it clear that some blanks should be filled with two- or three-word phrases, and some with single prepositions.

ANSWERS

The weather was so nice **in** the afternoon that I decided to go **for** a little walk **in** my new boots – the ones I'd seen advertised **on** TV as "the World's Best Boots." Well, **in** theory, they were very comfortable boots, but I soon realized that **in** fact they gave me blisters. Now, **in general** I enjoy walking, but by now I was **in** such pain that I was **in** a really bad mood. All I wanted was rest and refreshment. **In other words,** I wanted to sit down, have a drink, and return home **on the** / **by** bus. The last bus home was **in** half an hour, so I had to get to the nearest bus stop **in** a hurry. **At** last, the bus stop was **in** sight! I limped to the bus stop **in** the hope **of** getting on, but I was **out of** luck. The bus was completely full – not even standing room! I knew I'd never make it home **on** foot. I was **at** the point **of** giving up hope when another bus arrived, completely empty! I got on and sat down **at** / **in** the back. I began to feel **at** peace **with** the world again as I took off my boots!

Follow-up

1. Divide the class into pairs. They should have both pens and pencils at their disposal.
2. Have them write another story in pen but have them put all the prepositions in *pencil.*
3. Then they should erase all the prepositions and give the story with blanks to another pair to complete.

26.5   Finally . . .

Recommend that everyone highlight the phrases that were hardest to remember in this unit – more than ten if necessary. Students can then write their sentences for homework, to save time in class.

Afterward, have students look at each other's sentences, maybe copying a few of the best into their own notebooks.

Follow-up

To review this unit and the previous one:

1. Pick out about 20 sentences from the exercises – or adapt some sentences with your own ideas. Say the beginning of each sentence to the class and ask the students to complete it appropriately. For example:

Teacher: *The fire department arrived . . .*
Students: *. . . in the nick of time.*
                . . . because the house was on fire.
                . . . after I'd called them on the phone.
                etc.

2. Play a categories-type game. Divide the class into teams of 2 to 4 students. Draw a chart of five columns on the board. Choose five of these prepositions as column headings: in, for, by, on, at, out of, off, up to, under. For example:

In	For	On	At	Out of

(NOTE: The prepositions *off, up to,* and *under* are harder than the others because only one example for each is given in the Student's Book. You might use only one of these per round, perhaps as a bonus, if the competition heats up.)

The object of each round of the game is to fill in each column with a word or phrase from Unit 25 or 26. The first team to think of a *correct* phrase for *each* column wins the round and receives a point. As you go, list the winning choices on the board to take them out of play – only phrases that have *not* been previously used in the game are accepted.

SUGGESTIONS: (1) Change the headings around every few rounds. (2) For correct preposition + noun + preposition expressions give a bonus of a half point to encourage students to use them.

27 | *Reported speech: statements*

Grammar summary

Practice in reporting statements that were made recently (normally reported with present tense verbs):

"I'm feeling sick." → *She **says that** she's feeling sick.*
"It's too difficult." → *She **thinks that** it's too difficult.*

Reporting statements that were made some time ago (reported with past tense verbs):

"It'll be difficult." → *He **said that** it **would** be difficult.*
"It's a long way." → *He **told me that** it **was** a long way.*

Omitting *that* when reporting statements:

*She **says** she's feeling sick.*
*He **said** it **would** be difficult.*

Using a variety of "reporting verbs":

> announce   reply   add   tell   answer
> complain   explain   admit   suggest
> *They **replied** that they were feeling fine.*
> *They **told me** that I should be more careful.*

NOTE: If your students are confused about when to use *say* as opposed to *tell*, here are some brief, general guidelines:

1. Use *say* with direct quotations (when you are repeating a speaker's exact words) and reported speech:

DIRECT QUOTATIONS: *She **said**, "I'm having a party tonight."*
*She **said** to John, "I'm having a party tonight."*
REPORTED SPEECH: *She **said** (that) she was having a party tonight.*
2. Use *tell* with reported speech *when the person spoken to* is mentioned:

*She **told** John (that) she was having a party tonight.*
*She **told me** / **her** / **him** / **us** / **them** she was having a party tonight.*

Relevant errors

✘ He told me that he will do it yesterday.
✘ He said me that it was true.
✘ She told that it was true.
✘ She told me, that it was true.   *(punctuation)*
✘ They explained, I had to go with them. *(punctuation)*

27.1 What do you think?

Warm-up *(5 minutes)*

Look at the illustration as a class. Explain (or elicit from students) that the teacher has stated an opinion, and the student is reporting what his teacher said. Then look at the expressions to the left of the illustration. Ask students to report the teacher's opinion using these different expressions. For example:

According to her, it's wrong to cheat.
She thinks that it's wrong to cheat.
She believes that it's wrong to cheat.
She feels that it's wrong to cheat.

If students are comfortable using these expressions to report speech, you can go on to the procedure. If you feel they need more practice, ask a student to state an opinion (e.g., *Watching videos at home is more fun than going to the movies*), and then ask another student to report the opinion (e.g., *She thinks that watching videos at home is more fun than going to the movies*).

Procedure

A   In order to ask opinions of each other, students will have to circulate around the classroom. Encourage everyone to get three opinions on each topic. If time is limited, tell students to pick a set number of topics (e.g., five or eight) to ask about – they can then pick the topics that interest or amuse them the most.

Students will need to record the opinions, because they will have to report them to a partner in part B. Suggest that they record the opinions on a chart like this:

Not wearing a seat belt
Ana's opinion: Not important – doesn't
                       improve safety
Yoshi's opinion: Very important – saves lives
Luisa's opinion: Against the law not to – silly
                       to disobey the law

Cheating on an exam
Keiko's opinion: It's wrong
Giovanni's opinion: Sometimes it's OK – if
                       you don't get caught
Marie's opinion: It depends on the exam

B   *Pair work*   Reporting back can be done in pairs or in groups of 3. It may be necessary to get everyone started by giving the class an example:

One person I asked thinks that it's wrong to cheat on exams, but everyone else believes that it's all right as long as you don't get caught.

Ask each pair to tell the rest of the class which opinions surprised them most. (You may want to discourage the use of names when reporting opinions so that no one gets embarrassed; e.g., *One person said you should always wear a seat belt, even if you're only driving one block!* is preferable to *John said that you should always . . .*)

Follow-up

Have students list some more topics they would like to get their classmates' opinions on. Then have them ask each other, and later report to the rest of the class.

27.2   What did they say?

Warm-up   *(8–10 minutes)*

Look at the first set of illustrations. Point out that when the man reports the student's speech to the woman, the tense changes. Then look at the next set of illustrations, paying attention to the differences in tense between direct and reported speech. You may want to put the following chart on the board (perhaps leave the second column blank and elicit answers from students):

is	→ *was*
is doing	→ *was doing*
are	→ *were*
has done	→ *had done; done* (see remarks in the warm-up for Exercise 27.3)
will do	→ *would do*
may	→ *might*
can	→ *could*
must	→ *had to*

Then look at the first set of illustrations again. Note that the woman asks the man, "And what did you reply?" Ask students to report what the man said. For example:

He replied (that) he was sure she would.
He answered that . . .

Finally, to show how adverbs of time may change when we're reporting a conversation that happened some time ago, write this chart on the board:

now	→ *then*
today	→ *that day*
yesterday	→ *the day before*
next week	→ *the week after*
tomorrow	→ *the day after*
last week	→ *the week before*
here	→ *there*

Procedure

As a class, look at the exercise on the top of page 55 in the Student's Book. Encourage students to use a variety of reporting expressions when doing this exercise – they can use the list on page 54 of their books for ideas, as well as expressions of their own. Besides adding variety, words like *admitted* and *suggested* can also sometimes help to convey the mood and intention of the speaker. Point out, for example, that there are other ways of reporting Jim's second sentence and elicit some ideas from the class (e.g., *He added / explained that he didn't like thunderstorms*).

This exercise can be done in class, with students working in pairs or alone, or as homework. Point out that the conversation with Jim took place *some days ago.* You might want to do one sentence as a class to check that students change not only the tense but the adverbs of time as well.

Remind students that the word *that* can be omitted when reporting speech. For example: *He told me the sky was very cloudy that day.* Leaving *that* out is more economical when writing. However, in conversation, using *that* can be an effective way of hesitating while you think of what to say next. For example: *He told me that . . . the sky was very cloudy that day.*

SAMPLE ANSWERS

He admitted **that he got nervous if there was a thunderstorm.**

He told me / complained that the sky was very cloudy that day.

He added that it would probably rain later on.

He announced that he was going to take his new umbrella to work with him.

He explained that he had just bought it the day before.

He suggested that he could use it for the first time.

He told me that he hadn't had a chance to try it out yet.

He admitted that he wouldn't mind if it rained that day.

He added that he hoped that there wouldn't be any thunder or lightning.

He told me that if he heard any thunder, he'd stay indoors.

He admitted that he was a coward.

Follow-up

Look again at Jim's words in the Student's Book. This time ask everyone to report the *gist* of what he said (i.e., the main idea) in a few sentences, instead of reporting it word for word.

This can be done in pairs, or you could do this together on the board, with the class suggesting the most important points that Jim made.

There is no "best" way of doing this activity, but one way of reporting the gist might be as follows:

Jim told me he was afraid of thunderstorms and that he'd just bought a new umbrella which he hadn't used yet. He said he wouldn't mind if it rained later so that he could try it out, but he hoped there wouldn't be any thunder or lightning . . .

27.3 Communication activity: Guess what!

Warm-up

Begin by showing the class that we can use either the past perfect or the simple past when reporting a story someone else has told us. For example, if your friend Sandy said to you:

I got up late on Saturday and didn't have breakfast till 10 a.m. Then I went to the market to buy some groceries for my evening meal. I bought some fresh vegetables and I bought some fish. While I was there I met Karen.

it's much too complicated to report her story using the past perfect over and over, so usually we switch to the simple past fairly quickly:

Sandy told me that she had gotten up late on Saturday and didn't have breakfast till 10 a.m. Then she went out to the market to buy some groceries for her evening meal. She bought some fresh vegetables and she bought some fish. While she was there she met Karen.

Procedure

Pair work   Student A looks at Activity 32; Student B looks at 40. Student A reports a conversation he or she has had with Mary, while Student B reports a conversation he or she has had with Mary's husband, John. Look at the sample dialogue as a class.

Then ask everyone to read the passage in their activity silently. Tell students that during their conversations they can use the gist of the passage if they prefer, without reciting it word by word.

Encourage students to use the following expressions when they disagree with each other (perhaps write them on the board):

Oh, really?   *That's odd.*
How strange!   *Are you sure?*
You're kidding!   *That's funny, because . . .*
Hmm . . .

SAMPLE ANSWERS
These are rearranged roughly in the order they might occur in the discussion between Student A and Student B.

A: **Mary told me that she and John had been married for eight years.**

B: **That's funny, because John told me that he had only known Mary for six years. He said they had first met at a New Year's Eve party.**

A: **Really? Mary said she first got to know him at a friend's birthday party.**

B: **You're kidding! John said that they (had) first met at a New Year's Eve party.**

A: **That's odd – Mary told me that they had been introduced at a friend's birthday party. She said that he arrived at the party very late.**

B: **Hmm . . . John said that they both arrived at the party at the same time.**

A: **Mary added that John didn't recognize her when he asked her to dance, and that she first refused. But then she said they danced all night.**

B: **That's funny because John told me that they only had one dance.**

A: **You're kidding. Mary said that John was a terrible dancer.**

B: **How strange – John said that she had told him**

that he was great dancer but that she felt tired.

A: **Mary said that she told John that she didn't really want to dance.**

B: **That's interesting. John said that they sat down and started talking.**

A: **Mary said that they didn't leave the party till dawn.**

B: **John told me that they made a date to meet again the next week.**

A: **Really?**

B: **Yes, and he told me that they left the party separately.**

A: **Mary said that they went out together every evening that week.**

B: **I see. John told me that they seemed to get along very well when they met again.**

A: **Mary told me that they got married about six months later – on July 7th.**

B: **The 7th? But John told me that they got married on July 17th.**

A: **Mary said she would never forget their honeymoon: It rained all the time.**

B: **It rained? John said that they went to the Canary Islands for their honeymoon and that the weather was great.**

B: **John said that they had been happily married ever since.**

A: **Mary told me they had managed to stay together ever since – in spite of having fights almost every week!**

B: **Well, John told me that they hadn't had a single fight in all those years and that they were the perfect couple!**

Follow-up

Rearrange the pairs so that everyone has a new partner to talk to. Each pair should consist of one student who was looking at Activity 32 earlier and one who was looking at Activity 40.

Have pairs discuss what Mary or John told them again, again using reported speech. This time, however, they should use stress when they disagree with each other, rather than expressions such as "That's odd" or "You're kidding." For example:

A: *Mary said they'd been married for eight years.*

B: *No, John said they'd been married for* six *years. He told me they'd met at a New Year's Eve party.*

A: *Mary said they'd met at a* birthday *party.*

Note that the stress occurs on *new* information that is being introduced.

27.4   In other words

Warm-up *(2–3 minutes)*

Ask for volunteers to act out the dialogue in the Student's Book in front of the class. Alternatively, students can act out the dialogue in pairs.

Procedure

This exercise can be done in pairs in class, or as homework. Encourage students to use the verbs *agree, disagree,* and *deny* when reporting the dialogue.

SAMPLE ANSWERS

Ann told Tom (that) he had to do something about his hair. Tom answered (that) he liked having long hair, but Ann replied (that) she thought it looked ridiculous but Tom disagreed and said (that) it was the latest style. Ann replied (that) long hair on men hadn't been in style for years, but Tom claimed (that) he didn't care and (that) what mattered was whether he looked good or not. Ann told him (that) he looked awful, especially now that he was starting to go bald. Tom denied (that) he was going bald and explained (that) he just didn't have as much hair as he used to. Ann suggested (that) he was afraid to go to the barber's in case the barber laughed. Tom agreed (that) he hadn't been to a barber in ages, but then Ann interrupted him and offered to cut it for him herself. She told him to sit down. Tom told her (that) he didn't trust her. He said (that) he was afraid that she would cut it so short (that) everyone would think he'd just come out of the army! Then Ann said (that) she would just get some scissors . . .

Follow-up

The idea of this game (a version of "Chinese Whispers" / "Telephone") is for students to report a series of statements from person to person around the circle until each statement returns to the person who originally made it.

Arrange the class in a large circle – or if there isn't room for this, in two or three separate circles. The "circle" needn't be circular: It can even be rectangular as long as it's continuous.

In the first round, every alternate student (students 1, 3, 5, 7, etc.) makes a statement to the person on his or her *right* (students 2, 4, 6, 8, etc.). This statement is then passed on to the next person on the right. The sentences will probably change owing to misunderstandings as they travel around the circle. For example, the game might begin like this:

A (to B): *I didn't come to class last week because I had a cold.*

B (to C): *A said that he didn't come to school because he had a cold last week.*

C (to D): *A said he didn't come to school because it was cold last week.*

This goes on until the original statement gets back to A, who says it aloud:

You said it was very cold in this school.

In the second round, students 2, 4, 6, 8, and so on are the ones who make the statements to the person on their right in the same way. In round 3, students 1, 3, 5, 7, and so on have another turn, but this time saying their messages to the person on their *left*. In the final round, students 2, 4, 6, 8 and so on have another turn, this time saying their messages to the person on their left.

28 | *Reported speech: questions and requests*

Grammar summary

Practice in reporting *Yes/No* and *Wh-* questions (with a change in word order from direct speech):

"Is it true?" → *He asked me **if it was** true.*

"When is it going to happen?" → *He wanted to know **when it was** going to happen.*

Reporting requests, orders, advice, and invitations using *to . . .*

"Please open the door." → *She asked me **to** open the door.*

"You should stop smoking." → *She advised me **to** stop smoking.*

"Would you like to come?" → *She invited me **to** come.*

Using a variety of "reporting verbs" to report questions:

> *inquire   wonder   try to find out   want to know*
> *They **wondered** if I was feeling OK.*
> *They **tried to find out** where I lived.*

Using a variety of "reporting verbs" to report requests, orders, advice, and invitations:

> *advise   warn   try to persuade   invite*
> *want   encourage   remind   order*
> *urge*
> *They **warned** me not to do it.*
> *They **wanted** me to go with them.*

Relevant errors

✗ He asked me if I'll go there.
✗ She wanted to know when I did arrive.
✗ They asked when did you arrive.
✗ She asked me open the window.
✗ He encouraged me doing it again.
✗ She told him don't do it.

28.1   What did he want to know?

Warm-up *(3–6 minutes)*

Look at the illustration on the left and point out to the class how the man's direct question to the woman is transformed into an indirect statement in the illustration on the right. Ask the class to rephrase the indirect statement using some of the other expressions listed below the illustration. For example:

He wondered if I had finished my report.
He wanted to know if I had finished my report.
He tried to find out if I had finished my report.
He wanted to know when I would finish my report.
He wanted to know when my report would be finished.

Next write a few direct questions on the board. Then have the class transform them into reported speech. For example:

"Are you feeling OK?" →
   I asked her if she was feeling OK.
"What did you have for lunch?" →
   I asked what she'd had for lunch.
"Do you want to lie down?" →
   I asked her if she wanted to lie down.
"Shall I call the doctor?" →
   I asked if I should call the doctor.

Procedure

The exercise should be done in writing, either in pairs or alone. Ask students if they think the host and hostess were happy about the surprise visit – how would they feel if a friend unexpectedly came to stay with them?

Tell them that they can ask whatever they like, but if they need ideas Student A could ask about what B did last weekend, or last night. After a while, students should change roles so that everyone has a turn at being the mutual friend.

SAMPLE ANSWERS
(NOTE: As explained in the warm-up to Exercise 27.3, the simple past is sometimes used instead of the past perfect to report speech in the past tense, unless the past perfect is necessary to make the meaning absolutely clear. Both options are given in the sample answers where either tense is appropriate.)

They wanted **to know if I had had lunch.**
They asked me if I would like something to drink.
They wondered if I'd had any trouble finding their house. OR **They wondered if I had any trouble . . .**
They asked me why I hadn't phoned them.
They wanted to know how long I was going to stay.
They wondered if I would be able to stay till the weekend.
They asked me if I minded sleeping on the sofa.
They wondered why I hadn't brought my sleeping bag. OR **They wondered why I didn't bring my sleeping bag.**

Follow-up

Group work   Divide the class into groups of 3. Each group consists of Student A and Student B, who are "not on speaking terms"; They can only communicate through their mutual friend, Student C. For example:

A: *Ask him if he's all right.*
C: *She wants to know if you're all right.*
B: *Tell her I've got a headache.*
C: *He says he's got a headache.*
A: *Ask him if he wants an aspirin.*
C: *She wants to know if you want an aspirin.*
etc.

28.2   A very good day
Procedure

This exercise gives students a chance to review reported statements (Unit 27) before continuing further.

A   This part should be done in silence. Ask students to close their eyes and think about some of the places they've visited and things they've done recently. Allow a couple of minutes. Begin by saying: "Close your eyes and try to remember one particular day that was especially fun or memorable. What made that day special?"

B   *Pair work*   Divide the class into pairs or groups of 3. Students can make notes during this part to help them remember the information when they do part C. If the class needs ideas to answer the second question, give them some examples:

It might have been more enjoyable . . .
– if my best friend had come along.
– if the weather had been warmer.
– if I'd had more money.

C   The report can be written in class or as homework. Encourage students to use a variety of reporting words.

Follow-up

Form different pairs from the students who worked together earlier (in part B). They should tell each other what they found out in part B. If students wrote reports for part C, encourage them to avoid reading the reports to their partner. Rather, they should use their own words, referring to the report only to refresh their memory if necessary.

28.3   What did he ask you?

Warm-up *(2–5 minutes)*

Books are closed. Tell the class that they will be working in pairs and will have to ask their partner ten questions. If you anticipate that some students will lack inspiration, brainstorm a few questions that might be asked. For example, these could be very general:

What did you do last night?
Have you seen that new movie starring Michael Douglas / Harrison Ford / Tom Cruise / etc.?

Or more challenging:

What is your ideal job?
Where would you choose to live out of all the places in the world?

You could also list on the board several possible ways of beginning a question. For example:

Who ... ?   When ... ?   What kind of ... ?   How many ... ?   Is ... ?
Do ... ?   Did ... ?   Has ... ?
Would ... ?

Procedure

A *Pair work*   Books are open. Divide the class into pairs for these "interviews." Each student should answer the questions asked.

B   Now everyone changes partners and reports on the "interview." Go over the sample dialogue with the class first. Encourage students to reply to each other with remarks such as: *Oh, really? That's interesting. That's an unusual / interesting question. "Hmm ... And what did you reply?"* At the end, ask the class to report on the most interesting questions they were asked – and how they replied to them.

28.4   What did she want you to do?

Warm-up

Look at the illustration and examine how the woman's request was restated by the man. Then look at the examples beneath the illustration. Ask the class which of these expressions could have been used by the man to state the request. For example:

She told me / She wanted me to / She reminded me to call her.

Then ask the class to read the sentences in the left-hand speech bubble. They should imagine that a friend is speaking to them on the phone. When they have read the sentences, they should report what the friend said. Discuss the first sentence as a class, and ask for suggestions on other ways of stating it. For example:

She encouraged me/told me/wanted me/advised me to relax more.
She urged me to take it easy.
She told me I ought to try to relax.

Procedure

Students should do the exercise in writing, working in pairs or alone.

SAMPLE ANSWERS
(NOTE: There are many possible answers besides the ones listed here.)

She advised me not to **work so hard.**
She encouraged / urged me to get some fresh air.
She tried to persuade me to go out for a walk.
She warned / ordered me not to spend so much time studying.
She asked / urged me to come and see them soon.
She invited me to have dinner on Monday.
She urged me to come because they hadn't seen me for ages.
She asked / told me to get there before 7:30.

She reminded me to bring some dessert.
She advised me to write down her address.
She told me to call her if I got lost on the way.

Follow-up

Divide the class into pairs. Ask students to imagine they are advising their partners what to do and say in a job interview. (If your students are too young to know about job interviews, they could give advice about what to do and say if they're going out to dinner in an elegant restaurant.) For example:

You should wear nice clothes.
You shouldn't smoke during the interview.
It's a good idea to prepare thoroughly.

Everyone changes partners and reports on the advice they were given earlier. For example:

She advised me to wear nice clothes.
*She warned me not to smoke during the
    interview.*

28.5 Communication activity: In other words . . .

Warm-up (5–6 minutes)

Books are closed. Remind the class that they have been practicing how to change original words (direct speech) into reported speech. Explain that now they are going to do the opposite: that is, rewrite reported speech into words that might have been used in the original conversation. On the board, write this reported conversation between a teacher and a student:

I asked Mary for her homework, but she answered politely that she didn't have it. I was really surprised, because Mary always does her homework. Then she grinned, handed me her homework, and reminded me that it was April 1st.

(NOTE: In many countries April 1st is called April Fool's Day, a day when some people play tricks and practical jokes on each other.)

With the help of the class, rewrite the conversation in dialogue form. (NOTE: There are many different ways of writing this dialogue.) For example:

Teacher: *Mary, could I have your homework, please?*
Mary: *Oh, I'm very sorry, but I don't have it today.*
Teacher: *Really? Well, that's strange! You always do your homework.*
Mary: (Laughing) *Here it is! Remember, it's April first! April Fool's!*

Procedure

Set the scene for the activity – explain that Dan and Kathy are friends who were recently discussing Lucy, a girlfriend of Dan.

A *Group work*   Divide the class into groups of 4 or 5. Half of each group should look at Activity 29, while the other half looks at Activity 37. There are two different versions of the same conversation (Dan's version is in Activity 29 and Kathy's in 37), which students have to rewrite in dialogue form. Explain the procedure for part A carefully, making sure no one looks at the wrong activity by mistake.

The exercise practices rewriting reported speech into the original words that may have been used in direct speech.

SAMPLE ANSWERS
Activity 29 (Dan's version)

Dan: *You know, I'm dating Lucy.*
Kathy: *What? Call her right now and* **break everything off.**
Dan: **I can't believe this! You can't tell me how to run my personal life.**
Kathy: **Ha ha. Don't be so silly, Dan.**
Dan: **Get out of here and leave me alone!**
Kathy: **Don't take it like that. It's all for your own good. Let me explain . . .**
Dan: **I don't want to hear it. Just go away and let me run my own life, OK?**
Kathy: **OK, if that's the way you want it, I'll go. Goodbye.**

Activity 37 (Kathy's version)

Kathy: *What are you planning to do about Lucy, Dan?*

Dan: *I don't know. I have no idea.*

Kathy: **Listen, you have to make up your mind about Lucy.**

Dan: **Well, what do you think I should do?**

Kathy: **If you ask me, I think you should phone her and call the whole thing off.**

Dan: **Oh, I can't do that. It would hurt her feelings. But I guess you're right.**

Kathy: **Look – I'm sorry, but I've got to go. There are some things I have to do.**

Dan: **Oh Kathy, please don't go. Stay and talk with me awhile.**

Kathy: **Sorry, Dan. Goodbye.**

Dan: **Please stay a little longer . . .**

B   When everyone has finished rewriting the conversations, they show their version to the other half of the group and discuss the differences. Alternatively, the groups could read to, or act out their dialogues in front of, the whole class.

Follow-up

A   Form new groups consisting of students who rewrote the same versions in part A earlier (if they were looking at Activity 29 earlier, they should now be with different people who worked on 29). Have students look at each other's versions and compare the various sentences they wrote.

B   Have pairs of students act out the dialogues (both versions) in front of the class.

C   For homework, have everyone eavesdrop on a conversation (at home, on the bus, in a cafe, etc.) and write a report of it, giving the gist. Although the conversation they overhear may not be in English, the report must be!

29 Relative clauses

Grammar summary

"Identifying" relative clauses (also called "restrictive clauses") contain essential information. "Nonidentifying" relative clauses (or "nonrestrictive clauses") contain extra, nonessential information, which is sometimes added as an afterthought.

Make sure students are aware of the use of **commas** in writing these sentences: "Identifying" relative clauses don't use commas, and "nonidentifying" relative clauses do use commas.

Practice in using *who, that, which, where,* or *whose* in "identifying" relative clauses:

He is the man **who** *I told you about.**
He is the man **that** *I told you about.*
This is the book **that** *you need.*
This is the book **which** *you need.*
She's the girl **whose** *mother won the prize.*
He has two sons: The son **who** *is a doctor lives in San Francisco.*

*Some people prefer to use *whom* here, but this is more common in writing and not often used in conversation:
He is the man **whom** *I told you about.*
He is the man about **whom** *I told you.*

Omitting *who, that,* and *which* if they are the objects of an "identifying" relative clause:

He is the man I told you about.
This is the book you need.

Using *who, which, where, when,* or *whose* in "nonidentifying" relative clauses, which are set off by commas:

Her mother, **who** *is 67, likes candy.*
My house, **which** *is very old, is falling to pieces.*
The year 1812, **when** *Napoleon went to Russia, was very significant.*

Using *who* and *which* to connect sentences (as conjunctions):

She is very shy, **which** *I find surprising.*
I'm in love with Chris, **who** *is a wonderful person.*

Relevant errors

✗ The girl which is in my class wears glasses.
✗ The person, who answered the phone, was my sister. *(punctuation)*
✗ His mother who lives alone has gray hair.
✗ I saw Peter who waved at me. *(punctuation)*
✗ Everything what I told you is true.
✗ My car, what is in the garage, won't start.
✗ The letter which I sent it last week still hasn't arrived.

29.1 This is the man who . . .

Warm-up *(2–3 minutes)*

Books are closed. Bring in some pictures of famous people your students will recognize (e.g., Michael Jackson, Madonna, Julio Iglesias) and ask them to give sentences without giving each person's name. For example:

That's the singer who made the album and video Thriller.
He's the famous singer who owns a pet monkey.
He's the singer who's also a fantastic dancer.

Procedure

Books are open. Ask everyone to look at the illustration in the Student's Book (in silence) and to think of at least two more things that the women might say to each other. For example:

That's the man who / that asked me to marry him!

That's the man (that / who) I heard about on the news.

That's the man (who / that) my sister used to be friendly with.

He's the man who / that walked out on my best friend.

Write some of the sentences that were suggested by the class on the board. Draw attention to the interchangeability of *who* and *that* (when discussing a person), and the possible omission of *who* or *that* when it's the object of the adjective clause.

Follow-up

A   Have students working in pairs, or doing this activity as homework, write a dialogue between the two women in the picture, using relative clauses where appropriate.

SAMPLE DIALOGUE

A: This is the man who has asked me to marry him!

B: I can't believe it! That's the man I was telling you about!

A: Do you mean he's the man who was on the news last night?

B: Yes! They said he was the richest man in the world! He's the one who owns lots of oil fields.

A: I can't believe it! He never told me about all this!

B: I guess he's a man who can keep a secret!

B   Ask students to write down two or three more sentences, using *who* or *that*. Go around the class checking for mistakes. Write some of the more interesting or amusing sentences on the board.

29.2   Communication activity: What's her name?

Procedure

Look at the pattern conversation in the Student's Book. Then Student A looks at Activity 14, and Student B looks at 25. Students will each have some information to help them identify the women pictured on page 58 (see also below). Encourage everyone to follow the pattern during their conversations and take turns asking questions.

SAMPLE ANSWERS

A: What's the name of the woman who has curly hair?

B: Her name's Linda.

A: She's the woman (who / that) was in my class at school.

Linda   Kumiko   Carol   Sue   Beth   Maria   Erica

Jane

Figure 29.1

B: **What's the name of the woman who has long blonde hair?**
A: **Her name's Carol.**
B: **She's the woman (who / that) used to go out with my brother.**

A: **What's the name of the woman who rides a motorcycle?**
B: **Her name's Sue.**
A: **She's the woman (who / that) used to be a fashion model.**

B: **What's the name of the woman who plays tennis?**
A: **Her name's Beth.**
B: **She's the woman (who / that) went to the same school as me.**

A: **What's the name of the woman who's a flight attendant?**
B: **Her name's Jane.**
A: **She's the woman (who / that) used to be my sister's best friend at school.**

B: **What's the name of the woman who has a baby?**
A: **Her name's Maria.**
B: **She's the woman (who / that) used to work with my sister.**

A: **What's the name of the woman who plays the violin?**
B: **Her name's Erica.**
A: **She's the woman (who / that) used to sing in a rock group.**

Follow-up

1. Cut out some photos from magazines, showing a wide range of people (not just glamorous models). On the back of each photo write the real or an imaginary name of each person.
2. Quickly show the photos to the class, telling them the name of each person. Don't linger too long on each photo – otherwise the next part will be too easy.
3. Ask the class to identify each of the people by referring to their appearance. For example:

Teacher: *Which one was Mike?*
Students: *I think he was the one who is wearing a red sweater.*
          No, he's the man who's riding a bike.

29.3   Communication activity: What's it about?

Warm-up *(2–5 minutes)*

Books are closed. Some of the titles given in the Student's Book may be unfamiliar to your students. If so, go through the titles, asking the class to identify at least what sort of thing each title is: *Hamlet* is a play, *Don Quixote* is a book / story, *Cats* is a musical, and so on. (If in doubt, refer to the sample answers).

Procedure

Group work   Books are open. Student A looks at Activity 22, Student B at 36, and Student C at 44. Make sure they follow the pattern in the conversation on page 58 in the Student's Book.

SAMPLE ANSWERS
Activity 22

***Don Quixote* is (a book / story) about a man who has a dream of being a perfect knight.**
***Batman* is (a movie / cartoon strip) about a wealthy man who dresses as a bat and fights crime.**
***E.T.* is (a movie) about a creature who comes from outer space.**
***100 Years of Solitude* is (a book) about a family that / which experiences magical happenings in their South American town.**
***Tampopo* is (a film) about a widow who tries to run a noodle shop outside Tokyo.**

Activity 36

***Hamlet* is (a play / movie) about a prince who wants to kill his father's murderer.**
***Kramer versus Kramer* is (a movie) about a**

divorced husband who tries to raise his son by himself.

King Kong is (a movie) about an enormous ape that / which is captured on a remote island and brought to New York.

Dallas is (a TV show) about a family that / which lives in Texas and runs an oil business.

Frankenstein is (a book / movie) about a scientist who creates a creature that resembles a human.

Activity 44

Cats is a musical where / in which all the actors dress and act like cats.

Superman is (a movie / cartoon strip) about a man who can fly and has other superhuman powers.

Gone with the Wind is (a book / movie) about a rich family that is caught up in the American Civil War.

Sherlock Holmes is (a movie / book) about a detective who solved many mysteries based on very little evidence.

Romeo and Juliet is (a play / movie) about a couple who can't marry because their families hate each other.

Follow-up

Have students write down the titles of two of their favorite books written in their language and two of their favorite movies. Then ask students to summarize the story of each one to the whole class, or to the other members of a group of 4, using the pattern they followed in the communication activity.

29.4   My friend John, whose . . .

Warm-up (*4–5 minutes*)

Books are closed. Write on the board some examples of "identifying" and "nonidentifying"

relative clauses, and draw everyone's attention to the punctuation and use of *who, whose, where, when, that,* or *which.* For example:

Her brother, who works in Hollywood, lives in Beverly Hills.   (i.e., She has only one brother.)

My brother who works in Hollywood lives in Beverly Hills, but my brother who is a student lives with our parents.   (i.e., I have two brothers.)

My mother, who is an excellent cook, has written a cookbook.

Madame Butterfly, *which was written by Puccini, is a wonderful opera.*

The person who / that asked to see you said his name was Mr. Smith.

The car (which / that) I'd most like to own is a Mercedes.

Point out and demonstrate that nonidentifying relative clauses are often spoken as if they were in parentheses (i.e., with a short pause where the commas would occur in written English).

Procedure

Books are open. Students can write the sentences in pairs together or alone, with pairs comparing answers later.

SAMPLE ANSWERS

3. My oldest brother, **who** has a moustache, is studying architecture.
4. The man **(that / who)** I saw on television is a famous writer.
5. The day **(when / that)** we left on our trip was Friday the 13th.
6. The time **when / that** I broke my leg skiing is one of my worst memories.
7. The car **which / that** was stolen was a blue Toyota.
8. My car, **which** I've had since 1989, is a white Honda.
9. The airline **that/which** I took to Hong Kong had wonderful service.
10. The Hotel Tyrol, **where** I stayed when I was in Italy, was a really nice hotel.

Follow-up

Go through the sentences in the exercise, modeling how they are pronounced. Again, point out that "nonidentifying" relative clauses are often spoken parenthetically. Have the class read aloud after you and then to each other in pairs.

29.5   Connections

Warm-up *(3–4 minutes)*

Books are closed. Write these pairs of sentences on the board and help students use *who* or *which* to join them:

I met my old friend Luis. This made me feel happy.
- *I met my old friend Luis, which made me feel happy.*

Luis and I were at school together. That was many years ago.
- *Luis and I were at school together, which was many years ago.*

Luis had a big smile on his face. He shook my hand warmly.
- *Luis, who had a big smile on his face, shook my hand warmly.*   OR
- *Luis, who shook my hand warmly, had a big smile on his face.*

Procedure

Books are open. Students should write their answers in this exercise. If necessary, go over the example and the next couple of sentences as a class before students start writing. This can be done in pairs, or alone with students comparing answers in pairs afterwards.

SAMPLE ANSWERS
2. **Mary ate four ice cream cones, which made her feel sick.**

3. **I'm going to the mountains for my vacation, which I'm really looking forward to.**
4. **I went to see a movie about space monsters, which gave me nightmares.**
5. **We started talking to Kim, who told us about her adventures in the jungle.**
6. **I wrote them an angry letter, which made me feel much calmer afterwards.**
7. **I spent a long time with Tom, who was very helpful and gave me some good advice.**
8. **You'd better rewrite this letter, which you wrote too quickly and carelessly.**

Follow-up

Divide the class into pairs. Ask them to write some more pairs of short sentences, like the ones in the exercise. Then they should pass the sentences to another pair, who have to rewrite the short sentences as single, longer sentences.

29.6   In other words . . .

Procedure

This exercise can be written in class, or done as homework.

SAMPLE ANSWERS
2. The clothes **(that) she was wearing were old and dirty.**
3. The person **who gave me the message was wearing a brown jacket.**
4. *Casablanca,* **which is my favorite film, was made in 1942.** OR *Casablanca,* **which was made in 1942, is my favorite film.**
5. The person **who gave me a job is an old school friend.**
6. The woman **whose husband you were rude to is upset now.**
7. The computer **(that) I bought on sale doesn't work.**
8. Pete, **who helped me study for my history exam, is my cousin.** OR Pete, **who's my cousin, helped me study for my history exam.**

Follow-up

Have students write sentences using relative clauses. If they need inspiration, they could write about their favorite: *movie, album, book, celebrity, political leader, composer, singer, athlete, food, car.* For example:

Madonna, who started as a singer, is now a movie star as well.

Spinach pie, which is one of my favorite foods, is made with spinach, cheese, and a special crust.

30 | *Joining sentences – I*

Grammar summary

Practice in using different verb forms with *when* in time clauses:

*I **spoke** to him when he **arrived***
*I'**ll speak** to him when he **arrives.***
*I **started** my dinner when he **left** / **had left.***
  (He left, then I started eating.)
*I **had started** dinner when he **left.*** (I started, then he left.)

Using different time conjunctions in time clauses:

  as, until, by the time, whenever, while, as soon as, since, etc.
*She phoned me **as** I was having breakfast.*
*I always feel sick **before** an exam.*

Using conjunctions to join sentences in different ways:

*I've brought my umbrella **in case** it rains.*
  (precaution)
*I've brought my umbrella **because** it's raining.*
  (reason)
*You don't need an umbrella **unless** it's raining.*
  (condition)
*I've brought an umbrella **so that** I don't get wet.*
  (purpose)
*I've brought an umbrella **even though** it's not raining.* (contrast)

Relevant errors

✗ While I watched TV she phoned me.
✗ During I was watching TV she phoned me.
✗ I'm watching TV since 6 o'clock.
✗ After that I recognized him, I said hello.
✗ I'll speak to him when he will arrive.
✗ Because the bad weather, we decided to stay home.
✗ Although I don't like him, but I must say he is charming.

30.1 When . . .

Warm-up (*3–4 minutes*)

Ask the class to look at the three illustrations in the Student's Book, and make sure everyone understands the different time relationships that are shown.

– *I was eating my lunch when John came in.*
  (In other words, John came in to the restaurant as the woman was in the middle of eating her meal.)
– *I ate my lunch when John came in.* (In other words, the woman started eating lunch right after John came in to the restaurant.)
– *I had already eaten my lunch when John came in.* (In other words, when John came into the restaurant the woman was finished eating her meal.)

Procedure

Go through the first couple of sentences in the exercise as a class, asking for suggestions for different ways of completing each one. For example:

1. *When he heard the phone ringing, . . .*
   – *he got up to answer it.*
   – *he asked his roommate to answer it.*
   – *he was taking a bath.*

You may want to ask the class to explain each of their suggestions in other words, to make sure they understand the meaning.

Pair work After discussing the various possibilities, the pairs should write down their most amusing or memorable sentences. There will probably be variations from the sample answers.

SAMPLE ANSWERS
1. When he heard the phone ringing, **he put down his book and went to answer it.**
2. When he got to the phone, **it had stopped ringing.**
3. When it rang again, **he picked up the receiver and said hello.**
4. When he heard his fiancée's voice, **he was delighted.**
5. When she told him the news, **he didn't know what to say.**
6. When he had recovered from his shock, **he told her what he thought of her for treating him this way.**
7. When he hung up, **he decided to go jogging.**
8. When the phone rang again later, **he wasn't home.**
9. When we saw him the next morning, **he had recovered from the shock and was in a good mood.**

Afterwards have each pair show their sentences to another pair. Ask some of the pairs to read their sentences aloud.

Follow-up

Ask the class to suggest what the man's fiancée said to him and how he responded. If you have already covered Unit 27 (Reported speech: statements), encourage students to use reported speech: *She told him, She admitted, She said that, He replied, He asked,* and so on.

30.2   Rearrange the sentences

Procedure

Go over the example in the Student's Book as a class to make sure everyone understands what to do. (Some of the sentences can be completed in more than one way, as the following show.) Students should write the complete sentences on a separate sheet of paper, working either in pairs or alone.

ANSWERS
1. I held my breath as the door opened slowly.
2. I didn't leave the room until I had finished all my work. OR I didn't leave the room until they arrived.
3. I bought a new coat when I'd saved up enough money. OR I bought a new coat soon after the weather turned cold.
4. I used to get in trouble whenever I came home late.
5. I forgot to wash my hands before I had dinner.
6. I sent the package as soon as I found the address.
7. I had eaten all her candy by the time she came back.
8. I went on vacation soon after the weather turned cold. OR I went on vacation when I'd saved up enough money.
9. I waited patiently until they arrived. OR I waited patiently until I had finished all my work.
10. I was able to do the exercise once I'd found the answers in the back.

Follow-up

A   Ask the class to suggest some other ways to complete the half sentences on the left. For example:

I held my breath **while I waited for the exam results.**
I held my breath **while I was swimming under water.**

Students can also do this activity in pairs. Then form groups of 4 by combining pairs and have them compare sentences.

B   Explain to the class that the following sentences tell a story about someone who arrived late for work. Read the beginning of each sentence aloud, and ask students to complete it. Alternatively, you could write the beginning of each sentence on the board. Sample answers are given in parentheses.

1. Even though it was getting late, she couldn't leave home until **(she had breakfast / she had**

washed the dishes / she had listened to the news on the radio).

2. She read her mail before **(she left the house)**.
3. She walked to the bus stop after **(she'd had another cup of coffee)**.
4. She had to wait at the bus stop until **(the bus came)**.
5. She read the newspaper while **(she was waiting / she waited for the bus)**.
6. She had been waiting for half an hour by the time **(it arrived)**.
7. She continued reading the paper during **(the trip / the bus ride)**.
8. She jumped off the bus as soon as **(it reached her stop)**.
9. Everyone at the office gave her dirty looks when **(she walked in late)**.

8. **After you have finished / finish this exercise, you can have a short rest.**

Follow-up

Divide the class into pairs. Ask them to write a well-known story in three or four paragraphs (e.g., a national folktale or a children's tale, such as "Cinderella" or "Jack and the Beanstalk"). The paragraphs should include some of the time conjunctions practiced in this unit. Students should omit the title.

The completed paragraphs are shown to another pair, who have to guess the title of the story.

30.3   Join the sentences

Procedure

Look at the example sentence in the Student's Book as a class. Point out that the order of the clauses can be reversed, but this sometimes changes the emphasis. Usually a comma is unnecessary when the time clause comes after the main clause. For example: *I saw a suit at half the price after I had paid $200 for the same one.* If necessary, do one or two more sentences in the exercise as a class. Students should then do the exercise in writing, working in pairs or alone.

SAMPLE ANSWERS

2. **After I had reported that my passport was missing, I found it in my suitcase.**
3. **When / After they entered the house, they took off their hats and coats.**
4. **While she was in college, she made a lot of new friends.**
5. **Until he told me he was your brother, I had no idea who he was.**
6. **After I took the phone off the hook, I got a lot of work done.**
7. **Before you leave the house, make sure you lock the door.**

30.4   Just in case

Warm-up *(6–8 minutes)*

Write these column headings on the board:

Precaution
Reason
 Condition
  Purpose
   Contrast

Then look at the list of conjunctions given in the exercise in the Student's Book. Elicit a sentence using each of the conjunctions from the class, or supply a sentence yourself. Then write the conjunction under the appropriate heading on the board. For example:

I'm going to leave early in case *I get delayed on the way.*   (precaution)
I couldn't reach her on the phone because *the line was always busy.*   (reason)
I couldn't reach her on the phone although / even though *I tried several times.*   (contrast)
It's important to make notes in a lecture so that *you can remember what was said.*   (purpose)
I'm going abroad on vacation if / as long as / provided that *I can get a cheap flight.* (condition)
I can't go abroad unless *I have enough money.* (condition)

Procedure

As a class, look at the illustration and the first sentence, and make sure everyone understands what to do. Some of the sentences can be completed in more than one way. Students should work in pairs to complete them, discussing the various possibilities.

SAMPLE ANSWERS

2. He's wearing a hat **because** he doesn't want people to know he's bald.
3. I didn't go to bed **although / even though** I had an awful cold and a fever.
4. I'm going to study hard **so that** I'll pass the exam.
5. You can teach me to drive **if / as long as / provided that** you promise not to get mad at me.
6. I won't speak to her again **unless** she apologizes.
7. I'm going dancing tonight **even though / although** my ankle is swollen.
8. The town was flooded **because** it had rained so heavily.
9. We're going out for a walk **if / as long as / provided that** the weather stays nice.
10. I'm going to take some sandwiches **in case** I get hungry.

Follow-up

Divide the class into pairs. Ask them to write the first part of eight sentences, each using a different conjunction from this unit. For example:

I always carry a dictionary in case . . .
I usually write in ink although . . .

Then the sentences are passed to another pair, who have to complete them in their own words. For example:

. . . I need to find out the meaning of a word.
. . . I can't erase my mistakes.

30.5   In other words . . .
Procedure

Look at the first sentence as a class. Students can write the remaining sentences in class or for homework.

SAMPLE ANSWERS

2. Because the weather **was bad, the trains were late.**
3. Because **he was clumsy, he broke the teapot.**
4. Even though **they were lazy, they passed the test.**
5. She left early so that **she would catch her train.**
6. Although **she left early, she missed the train.**

Follow-up

With a more advanced class, look back at the sentences in Exercise 30.4 and discuss how they could be rewritten in the following ways:

1. She brought an umbrella **in case of rain.**
2. He's wearing a hat **because of his baldness.**
3. I didn't go to bed **in spite of / despite my awful cold and fever.**
4. I'm going to study hard **in order to pass the exam.**
5. (no change)
6. I won't speak to her again **without an apology.**
7. I'm going dancing tonight **in spite of / despite my swollen ankle.**
8. The town was flooded **because of the heavy rain.**
9. (no change)
10. (no change)

Grammar summary

Practice in connecting related nouns or pronouns with coordinating structures:

Both *Bill* **and** *his sister came.*
Bring **either** *soda* **or** *juice.*
Neither *Mary* **nor** *John came.*
None of *the family came* **except** *Jane.*

Using adverb phrases to link two separate sentences together:

She had a great time at the party. **Meanwhile** *I was at home studying.*
He left at 6:30. **Before that** *we'd taken a long walk.*
We had a wonderful meal. **Afterwards** *we had to do the dishes.*
I hate bananas. **That's why** *I never eat fruit salad.* (reason)
I love oranges. **Nevertheless,** *I hate having to peel them.* (contrast)
You could have ice cream for dessert. **On the other hand,** *you could have fruit.* (alternative)

Using adverb phrases to connect several sentences together in a paragraph:

In the first place, *I don't like cooking very much.* **In fact,** *I hate it.* **What's more,** *I find that spending hours in the kitchen is exhausting.*

Relevant errors

✗ Both they like her and her sister.
✗ I don't eat neither meat nor fish.
✗ He fell into the lake after that he was rescued.
✗ He fell into the lake luckily he was rescued.

31.1   Both . . . and . . .

Procedure

Look at the chart with the class and the sentences that accompany it. (The ✓ = likes, and X = dislikes.) Then ask for a few more examples, using the structures in the Student's Book. For example:

Both Sue and Tom like bananas.
Neither Ann nor Bill likes bananas.

Ann likes both potatoes and pasta.
Tom doesn't like either rice or potatoes.
Ann likes neither rice nor bananas.

Only Sue dislikes eggs.
None of them dislikes eggs except Sue.
Everyone except Bill dislikes rice.

A   Students work in pairs to make up more sentences about the people in the chart. Check the sentences for relevant errors before moving on to part B.

B   *Group work*   Divide the class into groups of 4 or 5. Group members find out about each other's likes and dislikes, and record them on a chart like the one in the Student's Book. For variety, students could make their own lists of food and drink to ask about (instead of the same foods listed in the Student's Book). Alternatively, they could talk about a topic other than food, such as sports or entertainment.

C   Students should work alone to write sentences about their group members, referring to the charts they made in part B. Depending on how much time is available, tell students how many sentences they should write. When they are finished, students should re-form groups and compare their sentences.

Follow-up

A   Ask students to tell the class the most surprising thing they found out about their classmates' likes and dislikes.

B   With a more advanced class, ask for additional sentences using these structures: *and so does* and *and neither does*. For example:

Ann likes meat and so does Tom.
Sue doesn't like meat and neither does Bill.

31.2   Communication activity: Uncles!

Warm-up (*3 minutes*)

Books are closed. Write these patterns on the board (they're also in both communication activities):

Both .... and ....
Neither .... nor ....
.... doesn't have either a .... or a ....

Give some examples about members of the class. For examples:

Both Yoshio and Kumiko wear glasses.
Neither Pedro nor Manuel has a beard.
Tony doesn't have either glasses or a moustache.

Procedure

Pair work   Books are open. Student A looks at Activity 41, while Student B looks at 46. Tell students to find out about their partner's picture and *draw* in the missing

details on page 62 of the Student's Book. This must be done by asking questions, not by looking at the partner's page, of course! At the end students should compare their artwork with the original pictures in their partner's activity.

Follow-up

Divide the class into pairs. Ask each pair to write down the names of some pairs of well-known people who have something in common with each other. Then pairs challenge the rest of the class to say what the people have in common. For example:

"Elvis Presley and James Dean."
– Both of them were famous.
– Neither of them is still alive.
– Both of them were born in the same year: 1931!
– Both Presley and Dean were in movies.

(This activity could be done as a kind of contest, in which points are awarded for the most correct responses.)

31.3   Fog at the airport

Warm-up (*2–3 minutes*)

Books are closed. Write *because* and *because of* on the board. Ask students to imagine they work for an airline. Their job is to explain to customers why all the flights have been delayed. Tell them to be imaginative and to suggest as many reasons as possible, using *because* and *because of*. For example:

All flights have been delayed because the air traffic controllers are on strike.   OR   Because the air traffic controllers are on strike, all flights have been delayed.
All flights have been delayed because of bad weather / heavy winds / snow / and so on.
All flights have been delayed because of heavy air traffic.

All flights have been delayed because there is ice on the runway.

Procedure

Books are open. This exercise can be done in pairs, or by students working alone and comparing answers in pairs later. (NOTE: There are many possible ways to join the sentences, using *because, because of, so, so that,* and other phrases used in Units 30 and 31.)

SAMPLE ANSWERS

2. **Amy and Paul started talking because they were waiting for the same flight.**
3. **She was feeling very hungry because she hadn't had any breakfast.**
4. **When he offered her a sandwich, she was so hungry that she accepted the offer.**
5. **They got along well because they both liked music.**
6. **They both enjoyed playing the piano.**
7. **Although he was much older, she found him very attractive.**
8. **Even though they had a big fight the next day, they decided to get married.**
9. **She enjoyed both his cooking and his company.**
10. **He never let her go out alone, so she couldn't meet any other men.**

Follow-up

Have students (working alone or in pairs) continue the story of Amy and Paul in writing, maybe explaining Amy's reactions to the last sentence: How did she feel about this? What did she do? What happened in the end?

While students are doing this, go around the class and check their work, offering advice as needed. Then form groups so that the pairs (or individuals) have a chance to read other students' versions of the story and compare them with their own. If necessary, collect the students' work at the end, and check it more carefully.

31.4   Solving problems
Procedure

Look at all the phrases listed in the Student's Book. If any are unfamiliar to students, either elicit a sentence from the class using the phrase or produce a sentence of your own. When everyone understands the phrases, divide the class into pairs and ask them to complete the sentences. Encourage them to find all the possible alternatives for each sentence. Go around the class offering advice and explanations as necessary.

SAMPLE ANSWERS

1. You can go by plane. **However, / But** if that scares you, you can take the train.
2. I thought the plane would be delayed. **That's why / So / Therefore,** I brought a book to read.
3. Everyone in my class got sick with the flu. **Believe it or not / Strangely enough / Luckily / Fortunately** I was the only one who didn't get it!
4. I discovered I didn't have any cash with me. **Luckily / Fortunately / However, / Nevertheless, / But** I had my credit card.
5. I knew it was likely to rain. **Nevertheless, / But / However,** we decided to have a picnic.
6. I just spent my last dollar. **In other words, / That is to say,** I'm flat broke.
7. Remember to take your passport. **Otherwise** you won't be allowed to cross the border.
8. They fell into the ocean. **Unfortunately,** neither of them could swim.

Follow-up

Divide the class into pairs. Have them pick the five phrases from the list that they think are the most useful for them and which they want to remember. Then they should write their own examples. For an additional challenge, have students write the linking words in each sentence *in pencil.* Then they erase the linking words and pass the sentences to another pair to fill in the blanks.

31.5   Communication activity: The reasons why . . .

Warm-up

Look at the phrases in the Student's Book and go over the example in the Pair Work section. Then ask the class to suggest more reasons why accuracy is important. Note the points that are made and then, with the class, continue the paragraph that was started in the Student's Book. Here are some additional reasons:

– *people may misunderstand you*
– *mistakes upset some people*
– *people may pay more attention to your mistakes than to what you're trying to say*

The paragraph might continue thus:

. . . What's more, inaccuracy can cause confusion and misunderstandings. In addition, mistakes may upset some people. Finally, people may pay more attention to your mistakes than to what you're trying to say.

Procedure

Divide the class into pairs. Student A looks at Activity 33 while Student B looks at 49. This is a discussion activity, so allow ample time. Note that the Communication Activity gives students some ideas for starters, but students should add their own reasons wherever possible. Encourage students to use the expressions listed on page 63 in the Student's Book.

If you think this activity is too difficult, the class can be divided into groups of 4 or 5. Then two students in each group can look at Activity 33 while the others look at 49, sharing the information there.

At the end, have students select one of the topics they discussed in the activity and write

two paragraphs about it – one showing the "pros" and the other the "cons." Encourage students to add their own ideas, besides those listed in their books. This can be done by students working together in pairs, or working alone.

Follow-up

A   Explain to students that, for homework, they're going to write a short story about "a walk in the country," beginning with one of these lines:

It was a glorious sunny day – a perfect day for a walk in the country . . .
George set off on his walk in high spirits . . .

and ending with one of these lines:

. . . If he'd known what was going to happen he'd have stayed in bed.
. . . It was the worst experience of his life.

Write the lines on the board and then brainstorm some ideas for writing the story before assigning the homework.

At the end, have students read and comment on two other students' stories before they hand them in to be marked.

B   Explain to students that, for homework, they're going to write a short composition about "the advantages and disadvantages of being a student," beginning with one of these lines:

Many people believe that being a student is . . .
It's not all fun being a student . . .

and ending with one of these lines:

. . . being a student only lasts for a few years, so it's best to enjoy it while you can.
. . . so although I try to study hard I also want to enjoy my freedom, while it lasts.

Write the lines on the board and then brainstorm some ideas for the composition before assigning the homework.

At the end, have students read and comment on two other students' compositions before they hand them in to be marked.

32 | *Word order*

Grammar summary

Practice in arranging modifiers (i.e., adjectives and other words that come before a noun) in the correct order:

(See bottom of page for chart.)

Placing adverbs in "mid-position" in a sentence:

*I have **never** eaten oysters.*
*I can **never** eat oysters.*
*I **never** eat oysters.*
*I'll **never** eat oysters.*

(Other "mid-position" adverbs are: *always, often, almost, hardly, rarely,* etc. – see Exercise 32.3 in the Student's Book.)

Using other adverbs which fit more comfortably at the beginning or end of a sentence:

Yesterday *I went to the zoo.*
I went to the zoo **yesterday.**
Recently *I traveled to Rome.*
I traveled to Rome **recently.**

Some of these also fit in mid-position:

*I **recently** traveled to Rome.*

It is best for students to rely on their own feelings for what sounds right or "comfortable," rather than try to memorize complex rules of word order.

Relevant errors

✗ Five winter black Italian coats.
✗ Never I have headaches.
✗ She fell nearly over.

✗ I yesterday went to the zoo.
✗ I shouldn't probably eat candy.

32.1 Modifiers

Warm-up *(3–5 minutes)*

Books are closed. If possible, bring a few interesting objects and/or pictures to class. Encourage students to brainstorm as many modifiers as possible to describe the item(s). If students need help, use prompts: "Tell me about the size / material / nationality / cost / color." List the modifiers on the board as they are suggested, without reference to order. Finally pose the question: "How could we put these modifiers in order?" Instead of answering, however, have students open their books to page 64 and figure out the answer. Work out the correct word order as a class.

Procedure

A   Books are open. Look at the examples in part A with the class and reassure students that phrases this long are not common in everyday English! Nevertheless, the rules they illustrate apply to shorter phrases:

an interesting science book
two large blue vans
a modern Italian coffee table

Answer any questions about the examples before going on to part B. The examples illustrate "rules of thumb"; however, it is

1	2	3	4	5	6	7
NUMBER	SIZE + QUALITY	COLOR OR PATTERN	NATIONALITY	MATERIAL	NOUN as modifier	NOUN
two	*beautiful*	*brown*	*Greek*	*ceramic*	*water*	*pitchers*

possible to use different word order to place emphasis. So, in the last example, if the speaker wanted to emphasize that the helmets were Japanese, the word order could be: *Four fantastic modern Japanese silver fiberglass motorcycle helmets.*

B   This activity can be done by students working in pairs, or working alone and then comparing answers in pairs later.

SAMPLE ANSWERS
1. **Five beautiful large black Italian winter coats**
2. **Six brilliant young Mexican film directors**
3. **Seven valuable white Korean ceramic flower vases**
4. **Eight beautiful pink Indonesian cotton tennis shirts**
5. **Nine lovely bright green Brazilian house plants**
6. **Ten strange wobbly yellow Swedish plastic bicycles**

Follow-up

A   Ask the class to work in pairs to produce two more similar examples, beginning: *Eleven . . .* and *Twelve . . .* Then they compare sentences with another pair.

B   Have students describe some objects in the classroom and their own or each other's clothes. This can be done orally as a class, or in writing as pair work. In this case, shorter phrases than the ones in the exercise are called for. For example:

There's a large green bulletin board near the door.
I'm sitting on a small wooden chair.
There's a large round table by the window.
Kumiko's wearing a blue knit cardigan and Italian leather shoes.

32.2   Adverbs

Procedure

A   Look at the examples with the class. Try to get students to share the "feeling" that, for

example, *I yesterday had a toothache* "feels wrong."

B   First make sure everyone understands the adverbs. Then students work in pairs and put the adverbs and adverb phrases into the sentences.

SAMPLE ANSWERS
2. She was waiting for me **indoors**.
3. **Tomorrow** he's leaving the country. OR He's leaving the country **tomorrow**.
4. She sings and dances **beautifully**.
5. **Once a week** they write to their parents. OR They write to their parents **once a week**.
6. I stayed in the library and worked **hard**.
7. The door opened **slowly** and a hand appeared. OR The door opened and **slowly** a hand appeared. OR The door opened and a hand appeared **slowly**.
8. He plays the piano **very well**.
9. You'll have to run **fast** to catch the train.
10. They hid the presents **behind the sofa**.

Follow-up

Divide the class into pairs. Have each pair write down five more sentences (without adverbs) and pass them to another pair. Then that pair has to insert an adverb into a suitable position in each sentence. Finally, the completed sentences with insertions are returned to their original authors.

32.3   Mid-position adverbs

Notes

1. A "mid-position" adverb usually follows the auxiliary verb, whether in a negative sentence or an affirmative sentence (but see note 2, following, for an exception). For example:

I have often drunk milk before going to bed.
I haven't ever had coffee before going to bed.
You should never drink coffee before going to bed.
You shouldn't ever drink coffee before bed.

2. The following adverbs are normally placed *before* an auxiliary verb in a negative sentence (but *after* it in an affirmative sentence): *obviously, clearly, surely, probably, presumably, certainly, apparently.* For example:

He probably hasn't been working hard enough.
She has probably been working too hard.
They certainly won't understand the book.
They will certainly understand the movie.

In both negative and affirmative sentences, adverbs can sometimes be placed at the beginning of a sentence:

Certainly they won't understand the book.
Probably she's been working too hard.

In affirmative sentences adverbs can be placed before the auxiliary verb, for emphasis:

They certainly will *understand the movie.*
She probably has *been working too hard.*

Warm-up and procedure

A   Go through the examples with the class. Make sure students notice that "mid-position" adverbs usually *follow* the auxiliary verb in a negative sentence (see preceding note 1), but mention the exceptions (see preceding note 2).

Write the following sentences on the board and have students decide where the adverbs in the list in the Student's Book can be inserted in these pattern sentences (not all adverbs will make sense in every sentence, of course, and not every appropriate adverb is listed in the following answers):

1. *Learning English is hard work.*
   Learning English is **often / hardly ever / clearly / apparently / really** hard work.
   Clearly / Apparently learning English is hard work.
2. *We have reached the end of this book.*
   Obviously we have **almost** reached the end of this book.
   We have **obviously** reached the end of this book.
3. *English grammar doesn't seem difficult to me.*
   English grammar doesn't **always / ever** seem difficult to me.
   English grammar **certainly** doesn't seem difficult to me.

4. *I enjoy doing homework.*
   Usually / Clearly I **rarely / frequently / really** enjoy doing homework.

B   This activity can be done in pairs, or by students working alone and then comparing answers in pairs later.

SAMPLE ANSWERS
1. I've **always** enjoyed Westerns.
2. I've **just** finished my work.
3. **Certainly** you'll be met at the airport. OR You'll **certainly** be met at the airport.
4. He **clearly** shouldn't have done that. OR **Clearly** he shouldn't have done that.
5. Oops! I **nearly** fell over.
6. We're **probably** going to be late.
7. I can **hardly** understand him.
8. She **rarely** loses her temper.
9. **Obviously** it's quite difficult. OR It's **obviously** quite difficult.
10. Things won't **ever** improve.

Follow-up

Divide the class into pairs again. Have each pair write down the beginnings of five more sentences, up to and including the adverbs. Each half sentence must contain one of the adverbs listed in Exercise 32.3A. Then students pass them to another pair who have to complete the sentences. For example:

I have almost . . .
– saved up enough money to go on vacation.

At the end, form groups of 4 by combining pairs so that students can see whether their sentences were completed according to their expectations.

32.4   Rearrange the words

Warm-up (*1–2 minutes*)

Books are closed. Write these words on the board and ask the class to rearrange them into a well-known saying and explain the meaning:

right   customer   The   always   is
The customer is always right.

– In the business world you should never argue with a customer.

Procedure

Pair work   When pairs have finished, discuss the meanings of the sayings.

ANSWERS

1. **The pen is mightier than the sword.** (Writing can be more effective than armed force.)
2. **If at first you don't succeed, try and try again.** (Don't be discouraged if you fail at something the first time. Keep on trying.)
3. **Rome wasn't built in a day.** (Time and patience are needed for a difficult undertaking.)
4. **When in Rome do as the Romans do.** (Adjust your habits according to the customs of the place you're living in or visiting.)
5. **It's no use crying over spilled milk.** (Don't waste time being sorry about mistakes that can't be changed now.)
6. **Every cloud has a silver lining.** (Good things can come out of a bad situation.)
7. **All good things must come to an end.** (You can't go on enjoying something forever.)

Follow-up

Ask pairs to think of some more sayings, rewrite the words in the wrong order, and then challenge another pair to arrange them correctly. For example:

*It   to   all   make   world   takes
kinds   a*
It takes all kinds to make a world. (It's good that there are many different kinds of people in the world.)

All's   that   well   well   ends
All's well that ends well! (We've come to a happy end after some difficult experiences!)